A Primer on Money, Banking, and Gold

A PRIMER ON

A Caravelle Edition

A DIVISION OF RANDOM HOUSE

MONEY, BANKING, AND GOLD

by *Peter L. Bernstein*

What is here?
Gold, yellow, glittering, precious gold?
. . . This yellow slave
Will knit and break religions; bless th' accurst;
Make the hoar leprosy adored; place thieves,
And give them title, knee, and approbation
With Senators to the bench . . .

Timon of Athens, *IV, 3*

VINTAGE BOOKS

NEW YORK

For my mother

Introduction

Baron Rothschild was once heard to say that he knew of only two men who really understood gold—an obscure clerk in the Bank of France and one of the directors of the Bank of England. "Unfortunately," he added, "they disagree." Most people would share his sense of frustration on the subject.

Disturbing questions about gold pursue us. Are we or are we not on the gold standard? Why have we been losing gold? Does the loss of gold mean that America is going broke? What has gold to do with money anyway? Where did Americans find enough money to write checks adding up to nearly four *trillion* dollars during 1963? Did the Government print it all? If not, how did it get onto the books of the banks? Why do some people worry that we have too much money—

how could anyone worry about too much money? But then we hear that others are concerned that we have too little; they want us to create more money. But how can we actually increase the supply of money? If we can do that, why aren't we all rich?

These are the questions with which this book is concerned, and we shall find that they are less difficult and complex than they appear. Furthermore, the informed citizen should, in any case, have a commonsense understanding of these matters. Indeed, most of his trouble in understanding them results from the knowledge that he *thinks* he has, because so much of it bears a superficial resemblance to his experience in handling his own affairs. But the thing is to have it right, to recognize and understand the difference between our own individual checking accounts and the great national accounts that influence the swing of economic events.

It is to this end that this primer is intended.

Contents

x) *Contents*

Part IV. GOLD

Part V. THEORY IN PRACTICE

A Primer on Money, Banking, and Gold

Part One

THE
MONEY PROBLEM

CHAPTER I

Why Worry About Money and Gold?

Everything that King Midas touched turned to gold, until ultimately he was a very poor man, because he had no useful possessions at all. The moral of this story is that money isn't everything in life. Indeed, money and gold bring wealth and power only in terms of what one can buy with them.

On the other hand, history tells us that money can be crucially important. Revolutions have seldom been caused by an excess of purchasing power, but men have frequently been stirred to violence when they are hungry and factories stand idle simply because no one seems to have enough money to buy what they are able to produce. Poverty in the midst of potential plenty always appears shocking and senseless.

These contrasts are the essence of the subject matter with which this book is concerned. Put in its simplest terms, we want to be sure that we have enough money around so that we can buy everything that has been produced, but never so much that we try to buy more than has been produced. The problem that will concern us most is the difficulty of keeping the number of dollars spent in line with the quantity of goods produced.

Despite the problems money causes, mankind invented it and sticks to it because it relieves us of the almost insurmountable difficulties of doing business through barter. For this reason, even the most primitive societies have tended to use some form of money, whether it be feathers or wampum or giant stones buried under the sea. As societies become more complex and people more specialized in the tasks they perform, money is even more necessary to enable one man to exchange his production for another's.

With the growing complexities of the marketplace and of the methods of production, we find that the character of money changes. It becomes more and more abstract, until it reaches the highly sophisticated form of our own money, which consists primarily of numbers on the ledgers of the banks that maintain our checking accounts. Although we still use some currency (worth, in reality, no more than the paper it is printed on) and some coins, most of the money we spend moves from buyer to seller through the writing of checks that order the banks to debit one account on their books and to credit another. Thus, most of our money has no real

value and no tangible existence: we can't see it or feel
it or smell it. This is one of the reasons why its quantity
is so difficult to regulate.

Nevertheless, while we shall be most concerned with
this abstract money that exists only on bank ledgers, we
shall also see that gold continues to play a crucial role
in our financial affairs. Sophisticated as we may be, our
links to gold persist. Gold has shown amazing vitality
through the ages as the paramount symbol of money
and wealth. The Midas legend teaches us that gold may
be nothing more than a useless (if beautiful) metal,
but it has surely been the cause of an extraordinary
amount of rapaciousness, plunder, and adventure in the
history of man.

Why gold is "good as gold" is an intriguing question.
Freud suggested that our fascination with gold is related to the erotic fantasies and interests of early child-
hood. Perhaps its very purity inspires men to violence.
Anyone who has ever seen a pile of gold bricks or gold
coins will always remember the sense of awe it inspires.
In any case, its prosaic physical characteristics—high
density and such strong resistance to oxygen that it
never tarnishes—have increased its usefulness as money.

Whatever the reasons, men will go to great lengths to
find gold and dig it up. After visiting the Klondike and
the Yukon, Will Rogers commented: "There is a lot of
difference between pioneering for gold and pioneering
for spinach." Although North American gold mines
are still producing, most of the free world's gold comes
from South Africa, where the white man owns and
profits from the gold but leaves to the black the business of digging it out of the dusty hell two miles below
the surface of the earth.

Yet, with all the digging and prospecting and plunder, men have managed to scrape together a surprisingly

small amount of this precious stuff. The entire accumulation of monetary gold over the centuries has brought the world's gold hoard today to just about 40,000 tons; American industry pours 40,000 tons of steel in less than one *hour!*

While nature essentially controls the quantity of gold in existence, it is men who assign it values in terms of dollars and pounds and rubles; it is also men who decide how much money a given amount of gold may "back." When we look at the alternations between inflation and deflation in our history, men seem to have done a poor job of regulating the supply of money.

We find repeated cases in which people seemed to have so little money that they were unable, or certainly reluctant, to buy everything that could be produced. As a result, prices fell, profits vanished, production shrank, and unemployment spread. Only when all prices and all wages had been pushed down so low that the formerly inadequate supply of money seemed sufficient to buy up all the goods and services offered for sale at bargain levels did the wheels finally begin to turn again and men go back to work.

We can also find frequent examples of the opposite situation—the inflationary spiral in which the quantity of money outruns the supply of goods. When people want to buy more than has been produced, prices rise. Then some people lose out through being outbid in the market place. Those who suffer most are usually the ones who least deserve to be the losers—the frugal, the conservative, the prudent, together with the poor and unorganized who are unable to battle for the higher incomes they need to stay even with the rising prices.

Thus, regulation of the supply of money is not just a matter that concerns financiers and bankers: it is intimately involved with our prosperity and with our social tranquillity. With all its technicalities, this is a subject with the broadest political and economic implications.

Our analysis of it now begins with the very crux of the process—the links that exist between the quantity of money and the levels of business activity and prices.

CHAPTER II

Spending and Financing

It is obvious, but nonetheless true, that each of us goes to work to help in turning out goods and services in our economy not for our own use, not out of the kindness of our hearts, but because we expect to sell the fruits of our efforts to other people, and because we expect to be paid for them.* In short, we work for money.

If this is the case, however, businessmen must have the money to pay their workers and suppliers for producing the goods they want to sell, and customers must have the money to pay for the goods they want to

---

* The labors of the housewife are an important and outstanding exception to this general proposition. Outside of her domain, little work or production is undertaken in our economy unless some one receives money for it.

buy. Without the wherewithal to pay for them, few goods would be produced and fewer would be sold. This leads, in turn, to the important conclusion that an increase in production or the sale of the same quantity of goods at higher prices simply cannot be sustained *unless people are willing and able to lay out the extra money they will need* to buy the additional goods or to pay the higher prices for the same quantity of goods.

Take, for example, the case of a family that has been spending $6000 a year on the basketful of goods and services it requires to maintain its living standards. Now let us assume that we enter into an inflationary phase and, as a result, the price of the same basketful rises from $6000 to $6600. To maintain its living standards, this family is now going to have to find an additional $600 every year. Where can they find it?

The breadwinner in the family—most likely, the father—can go to his employer and demand an increase in wages. But then, of course, the employer has to find an additional $600 a year to keep his employee happy. This money must either come out of his own profits from the business (in which case he will have less money to spend) or he must raise his prices and ask his customers to pay it. In that case, the customers must find the additional $600, and we are right back where we started.

If the father of the family is unable to obtain a raise from his employer, he still has several alternatives available to him. He can draw down money that he has accumulated in the past—the cookie jar can be emptied and its contents used to maintain the family's standard of living. He can go to the savings bank and ask them to give him back the money he previously deposited— but then the savings bank has to be sure it has the money. He can borrow the money from friends or from a finance company, but they, too, must have the money available to lend him.

And what if this family is unable to find the additional $600 it needs to carry on? Clearly, it will have to cut down on the quantity of goods and services it buys. If it can only afford to spend the same $6000, approximately 10 per cent of the things it bought before will now remain unsold. Retailers, finding that sales are falling below expectations and that inventories are piling up on their shelves, will cut down their orders from wholesalers. Wholesalers will tell manufacturers to ship a smaller quantity of goods. Manufacturers will then have to cut back on their production schedules; their employees will probably be laid off or will work fewer hours.

In time, then, the inability to finance the purchase of goods at higher prices results in unemployment and excess productive capacity. The forces of competition at work when businessmen can produce more than they are able to sell will probably lead to the elimination of the price increase. Or, if people are willing to pay for those goods whose prices have been raised, they will have less money to spend on other goods and services, so that unemployment will spread into those industries whose market power is weakest.

Just as an increase in prices must be financed if unemployment is to be avoided, so must an increase in production be financed if it is to take place at all. Here, for example, is a manufacturer of pencils, who is producing and selling 100 million pencils a year for a total of $1,000,000 in sales. He finds that business is excellent and that his dealers are reordering his pencils with increasing frequency. He therefore decides to step up his production schedules and to produce an additional 10 million pencils on which he expects to generate $100,-000 in extra sales in the coming year.

But first he is going to have to look around for the money to finance the additional production. He will have to obtain extra amounts of wood, lead, and rubber. He may need new workers or will have to pay his present staff for overtime work. He may even need a new plant or additional machinery. One way or another, he will have to find some way of paying for this expansion, since his customers, whether retailers or wholesalers, will probably pay him only thirty days or so after receiving the merchandise he has shipped to them.

He has a number of alternatives. He may have enough money sitting in his checking account to cover all the extra disbursements he must make. He can ask his suppliers, and possibly even his employees, to wait to be paid until after his customers have paid him. He can draw down his savings account or sell to other investors some financial asset he may possess, such as a short-term Government security or commercial paper. He can borrow the money, or he can take new investors into the business with him.

Thus, money that has to be spent must come from somewhere—either from one's own cash balance or from somebody else's money holding. And that somebody else either has to have the money himself or must be able to find still another source to provide it when needed. Unless the pencil manufacturer's suppliers and employees are to be paid—and, ultimately, unless the manufacturer's customers are going to be able to find the money to pay him—the extra 10 million pencils will never be produced.

Indeed, money makes the world go round.

. . .

The significance of this example is that the supply of money does set limits to how far business expansion can go and how high prices can rise. Both increased production and the same volume of production sold at higher prices involve a higher rate of spending by customers, and, when they have to pay out money, money is the only thing they can pay out. No bill can be paid with Government bonds or shares of stock or jewelry, or even a savings account or life insurance policy. Only a check or currency or coins will be acceptable for this purpose.

Nevertheless, although the supply of money can set the upper limit to a price inflation or to growth in production, we have no ready way of knowing where that limit may be. In fact, the *number* of dollars in our bank accounts and pockets is only an indirect, and frequently unsatisfactory, guide to the rate at which we are going to *spend* those dollars. And it is expenditure that counts —it is expenditure that comes into the marketplace to be matched against the supply of goods and services.

The relationship between the quantity of money and the rate of expenditure is so tenuous and variable because of a peculiar characteristic of money—a characteristic that it need not have in theory, but with which we have endowed it. Indeed, without this feature, money would be a much less convenient medium of exchange than it is.

The point is that we need not spend money the instant we receive it. We can take it in payment for something today but wait until the day after tomorrow to spend it. Or, in fact, we can let some one else use our idle dollars for a while, provided they will pay us an adequate rate of interest for the privilege of using our extra cash. But no law tells us that we have to spend every penny we earn, nor that we need spend it today instead of tomorrow, nor that we have to lend it out to someone else if the interest he will pay seems inadequate. In short, some production may go unsold simply because individuals and business firms sit on their money instead of spending it or making it available to others to spend.

Of course, the opposite can also happen. As we saw in the case of the family spending $6000 or in the case of the pencil manufacturer, we can step up our rate of spending merely by using some of the idle cash that we may have accumulated in the past or by finding others who may now be willing to make their cash available to us to spend. The man who borrows money or draws down his savings account to buy a house or a car, and the respected corporation that borrows money to finance its expansion programs are both spending in excess of their current incomes. When people spend more than they earn producing goods and services, the chances are that they will be trying to buy more than has been produced. This excess demand will then either stimulate an increase in production schedules or an increase in prices.

Thus, the rate of spending can vary widely, even when the supply of money in the economy is relatively stable. Conversely, variations in the supply of money will not necessarily lead to corresponding changes in the sales of business firms. Sometimes people want to accumulate cash rather than spending it or making it available to others to spend; at other times, they are eager to spend their cash hoards or to borrow and spend the cash hoards of others.

To recapitulate, we have seen that our main problem is to keep the rate of spending in line with the production of goods and services—neither so low that prices and demand collapse nor so high that an inflationary spiral begins. But we have also seen that increases in spending must be *financed*—that the additional dollars must come from the spender's past accumulations or be made available to him by others. And now we find that the ease or difficulty of financing a higher level of expenditure is only indirectly related to the supply of money: people's motives for holding, lending, and spending money are seldom constant.

No wonder, then, that we have been so unsuccessful at keeping expenditure in line with production. Controlling the supply of money in the economy is a partial, but by no means certain, technique for achieving our objective. Before analyzing the factors that do determine the number of dollars in existence, then, we must first have a look at the reasons why people want to hold onto more money at some times than at others.

CHAPTER III

The Price of Money

The most obvious reason for holding money is that we need it to pay for the things we buy. Most of us spend money at a rate different from the rate at which we earn it. If we should earn $15 a day and spend $15 a day, we would never have to hold money for more than a few hours. But since money comes in to most of us at regular intervals, whereas money is spent in amounts that may vary widely from day to day, we must have some funds available to finance our outlays during those periods when more is going out than is coming in.

Most of the money we hold, then, is for this purpose. And the more we spend, the larger the cash balances we will need to finance these expenditures. This also means that the higher the level of business activity and the more active the volume of production and employment, the more each of us will need the money we have and the smaller the amount we will be able to make available to finance the expenditures of others. For these reasons, we frequently hear that money is "tight" (that is, in tight supply) when business is good and that money is "easy" (that is, easy to obtain) when business is slow.

But most people and most business firms tend to carry a little more money than they absolutely require to finance their various transactions. If we earn $100 a week and spend $100 a week, we still try to keep enough money in our bank account so that our balance at the end of the week, just before payday, is something more than zero. This has been called the "precautionary" motive for holding money. You never know what might happen that would require the unexpected outlay of funds—an emergency, an unusual opportunity, a bargain sale, an irresistible hat or necktie in a shop window.

Yet, if you conducted a careful survey of all individuals, business firms, institutions, state and local governmental units, and other spending units in the economy, you would find some of them—and perhaps many of them—carrying currency or balances in their checking accounts in excess of what they need to finance their current expenditures, expected and unexpected. Why, then, should anyone let money sit in this way, earning nothing? It seems a wasteful and expensive way to manage one's affairs.

If it seems wasteful for someone to carry more cash than he needs, instead of putting it out to work to earn interest and dividends, that is precisely the point of the argument. We will indeed put our excess cash out to work *if the price is right*—in other words, if the return we will earn from the person using our money is *adequate* to compensate us for the risk and inconvenience of giving up this cash.

Of course, few individuals and business firms ever lend their excess cash directly to someone else. Instead, they put it to work through some sort of financial institution—a savings bank, insurance company, investment trust, or pension fund—that invests it for them, or they go into the security markets and buy marketable obligations issued by major corporations or governmental agencies. Furthermore, most of these marketable securities that are bought and sold each day are not issued by the borrower on that particular day but, rather, were originally issued at some point in the past. Thus, instead of being new borrowings that investors are putting their money into, these are securities sold by other individuals and business firms wishing to replenish their holdings of cash and liquidating these securities in order to do so.

In our highly developed and sophisticated financial system, this process of bringing together people with excess cash to invest and those who need additional cash to spend is institutionalized in what we call the "money and capital market." The money and capital market is not located in one particular place, like the stock exchange on Wall Street or the grain pit in Chicago. It includes the organized security exchanges, as well as the intricate network of relationships among nearly 14,000 commercial banks, 500 savings banks and 6000 savings and loan associations, the life and casualty insurance companies, the Federal Reserve Banks, and all the various dealers and brokers who buy securities from and sell them to these financial institutions.

Many less-developed nations have not yet been able to mobilize such an efficient mechanism for bringing

together the man seeking financing and the man looking for a spot to put his money to work. These countries consequently need a much larger quantity of
money than we do to finance a given volume of business: since no ready means exists to obtain additional
cash when one needs it, each individual and business
firm has to carry excess cash to be certain that it
can provide for its future requirements. This situation
also means that it is difficult to persuade anyone to part
with excess cash and that interest rates, as a result, are
significantly higher than they are in the United States
or Western Europe.

But let us return to the main thread of our argument.
We have stated that we would be willing to part with
our excess cash when the interest we receive is adequate,
but what do we really mean by "adequate"? Since any
amount of interest that we can earn on our money is
better than earning nothing on it, why should we turn
down, say, 1 per cent and insist on getting 4 per cent?
Obviously, 4 per cent is *preferable* to 1 per cent, but if
1 per cent is all we can get, that is still better than 0 per
cent.

One very simple explanation of this is that we just
don't want to go through the inconvenience of putting
money to work in order to earn nominal amounts. Although it may be irrational to turn down 1 per cent
when 1 per cent is so obviously more than 0 per cent,
we may still feel that 1 per cent fails to justify the trouble involved in putting our money to work. We will
choose, rather, to let the money sit in our checking accounts or in our pockets.

But a more important and compelling reason for
wanting to receive a high rate of interest is that, in ad-

dition to inconvenience, risk is involved in letting someone else use our excess cash. For one thing, he may not
repay when he promised, and we therefore deserve some
compensation for the credit risks involved. Furthermore, what happens if we want our money back before
the time that the borrower has promised to return it?
Will we be able to find another investor who will be
willing to take this obligation off our hands and give us
our money when we need it?

Thus, time horizons are crucial in influencing our
decisions to part with excess cash and in determining
our attitudes as to whether any given rate of interest is,
in fact, "adequate" for our purposes.

Indeed, investing money too soon when interest rates
are rising can be an expensive and frustrating business.
For example, the United States Government was able
to borrow money in 1953 for thirty years by offering
3¼ per cent to the buyers of its bonds. But, as business
activity expanded so much faster than the available supply of money in the years that followed, by 1959 the
Government had to offer lenders more than 4 per cent
interest in order to persuade anyone to buy its long-
term bonds.

This hardly left the buyers of the 1953 bonds in a
happy mood. These 1953 bonds paid $32.50 in interest
for every $1000 invested in them, while bonds issued
in 1959 paid over $40 on an investment of the same
amount. Consequently, if a holder of the 1953 bonds
needed his money back and therefore wanted to sell his
bonds to some other investor (he *had* to find another
investor, as the Government had no obligation to return
his money until 1983), he was unable to find anyone
willing to pay him $1000 apiece for them. As a matter
of fact, in the summer of 1959 investors were willing to

pay only $820 for one of these 3¼ per cent bonds.*
Over the six-year period the original buyer held them,
his $195 in interest (six years @ $32.50) would have
been largely offset by his capital loss of $180, so that his
actual return would have been only $15, or $2.50 a year
on an investment of $1000. A poor piece of business,
indeed!

But it can also be unwise to wait indefinitely for
lenders to be willing to pay us what we believe to be
an "adequate" rate of return for the use of our money.
For example, 1 per cent should appear "inadequate"
only if we have a genuine hope and expectation of actually receiving more than that at some point in the
foreseeable future. If we honestly believe that lenders
will never be willing to pay us more than 1 per cent, or
if we would have to wait an intolerably long time before we could persuade them to pay us more than that
amount, we would do well to take 1 per cent and make
the best of it.†

Speaking generally, the demands of borrowers are
determined primarily by their own expectations of us-

---

* The investor who bought the bond for $820 received $32.50
a year in interest, so that his rate of return appears to have been
about 4 per cent. However, if he held the bond until the Government paid it off in 1983, he would receive a full $1000 at that
time, or $180 more than he paid for it. The combination of the
current payment of $32.50 a year and the profit accruing between
the date of purchase and the maturity of the bond work out to an
interest yield of 4.45 per cent a year.

† In reality, for reasons already explained above in connection
with the risk that the lender may need his money back before the
borrower is obligated to repay him, evidence exists to suggest that
most people are unwilling to lend money for long periods of time
unless they can expect to receive 2 to 2½ per cent a year as a
minimum rate of return. This is no new idea. The famous nineteenth-century English economist Walter Bagehot quoted an old
saying that "John Bull can stand many things, but he cannot
stand two per cent."

ing money profitably, so that the price they will be willing to pay for the use of other people's money will tend to rise when business is good and production is expanding, and will fall when the outlook is dim and output is shrinking. Although many people consider low interest rates desirable because they make borrowing money more attractive to businessmen and will therefore stimulate business activity, history tells us that periods of high and rising interest rates, rather than low and falling interest rates, have been associated with vigorous and sustained prosperity.

Probably the most important point to be made in this discussion of motives for holding money or being willing to lend it out is that what *one* of us wants to do or succeeds in doing in these directions may be different from what *all of us together* may succeed in doing. If all of us need to carry more money in our bank accounts to finance our expenditures, only some of us may actually be able to do it; if all of us have more than we need and want to carry less, some of us may in fact end up carrying more!

The reason for this paradox is that one man's payment is another man's receipt. Money doesn't disappear after it is spent—its life continues in the possession of the person to whom it is paid; conversely, if one wants to build up the balance in his bank account, that additional money must be paid over to him by other people.

What, for example, would happen if we all decided to go out on a spending spree and spend all the money we had? Would we completely deplete all the balances in our collective checking accounts? Would we all go broke? Of course not, for we would continuously replenish one another's bank accounts. What I spent, you would get and what you spent, others would get. Of course, one of us could go broke if he spent all his money; nevertheless, at the same time he would be enriching the people to whom he paid his money out. When all is said and done, then, the rate at which we spend our money doesn't make the total supply of it any smaller or larger.

This also means that, collectively, we would get no richer if we all decided to spend nothing and to hoard all the money we held. Then no money would change hands, and everybody's balance at the end of this period of abstinence would be the same as it was at the beginning. No one would have any more, no one would have any less; no one would be any richer, no one any poorer. In particular, no one could increase the amount of money he held, because he could find no one else willing to part with any cash for his benefit. Thus, while *one* of us can take in more than he pays out but thereby depletes the cash balances of other people, *all* of us together cannot take in more than we pay out, because the money we take in must be paid out to us by other people. If none of us is willing to see his cash balance depleted, then none of us will be able to have his cash balance increased.

It is just these struggles for increased "liquidity"—for more cash on hand—that have led to repeated monetary crises in our history, of which the experience of 1929–33 was a dramatic, but by no means isolated, example. In that panic, everyone was a seller and no one a buyer. These instances are the culmination of a long process that begins when people who need more cash are at first able to get it by offering higher rates of interest for it; ultimately, no one has any more extra cash to lend out at any price. The panic sets in when people recognize that he who parts with cash today will have a hard time getting it back tomorrow.

In short, our collective decisions to hold more money or less can have no influence on the total amount of money that all of us together actually hold. When interest rates begin to move, that is a signal that the demand for money and the supply of it are out of kilter. Rising rates indicate that some people with too little cash are now willing to pay a higher price for the use of the other fellow's money, whereas declining rates show that some people are holding more cash than they need and are now willing to take a lower price to put it to work.

But this also means that the supply of money available for us to spend, lend, and borrow is a crucial factor in determining how much spending will actually take place. Since the objective of managing our national money supply is to keep spending more or less in line with the quantity of goods and services being produced, we must now turn our attention from the manner in which people use money to the process that results in the creation of the money that we actually use.

Part Two

THE CREATION
OF MONEY

CHAPTER IV

Money in Hand and Money in the Bank

When we look back over the past, we see wide fluctuations in the quantity of money in the United States. We had only a little more than 20 billion dollars in our checking accounts and in currency and coin in our pockets at the end of World War I and nearly 30 billion dollars in 1929; we dropped below 20 billion dollars at the depth of the Great Depression and then zoomed to more than 100 billion dollars by the end of World War II; today the figure is close to 150 billion dollars.

How could money actually have disappeared during the Depression? Where did those tremendous sums come from during the 1930's and 1940's? Why has the growth in the money supply slowed so much in the postwar years?

Before answering these questions, we should note first that the money we use takes two forms—coin and currency that we can see and hold in our hands, and checking accounts, which have no tangible existence at all and are only bookkeeping entries at commercial banks. One passes readily from hand to hand; the other moves in a devious and mysterious process through bookkeeping machines and electronic computers. These two forms of money, one visible and the other invisible, come into existence in different ways and have differing impacts on the way in which the system operates. We would do well, therefore, to consider them separately.

First, what causes the supply of coin and currency in circulation to go up and down? Since coin and currency are issued by the Government, the obvious answer to the question must be that the Government simply coins more coins and prints more currency and then "issues" them.

But this isn't what happens at all. In fact, some of the most serious misconceptions about our monetary system arise from failure to understand the factors that determine the amount of currency actually circulating from hand to hand.

Let us begin the story with the Government, however. In the course of a year, the Federal Government spends approximately 100 billion dollars on paper clips, atom bombs, salaries of Members of Congress and Justices of the Supreme Court, benefits for farmers, grants-in-aid to the states, Social Security benefits, and so on. In addition to these huge sums, the Government must also disburse additional billions (about 9c billion dollars in 1963, for example) to holders of Government obligations that come due during the year and have to be paid off.

The Government does make payments in the form of currency to most soldiers, sailors, and airmen. A few other salary and wage payments are made in currency. But for most recipients of Government payments, currency would be extraordinarily inconvenient to handle. Would the North American Aviation Company, which sold nearly 2 billion dollars of defense products to the Government in 1963, have wanted to handle such large sums in currency and coin? How about the cabinet officer who receives $25,000 a year? The old-age pensioner living in Kansas would worry about currency being shipped through the mails if his pension were paid in that form. The life insurance company holding 5 million dollars of maturing Government bonds surely does not want to be bothered with such a barrelful of money.

What this means, then, is that the Government has little or nothing to do with the amount of currency in circulation. Indeed, even if the Government did go to the trouble of paying out all these many billions in currency and coin, most of the individuals and business firms and state, local, and foreign governments receiving that money would turn right around and deposit it in the nearest bank as fast as they could. No one wants to assume the risk and inconvenience of having so much money around.

In this connection we might take a look at the famous stories about people running around with wheelbarrows full of currency during hyperinflations, such as the terrible experience of the Germans after World War I.

There, as in the Confederacy during the American Civil War and in France during the Revolution, the Government did print and spend tremendous amounts of money. In those cases, however, the use of checking accounts was either nonexistent or much less prevalent than it is today; currency and coin were the primary rather than the minor form in which money was handled. It was natural, therefore, that an increase in the total supply of money should have been reflected largely by an expansion in the amount of currency and coin in use.

But the part about the wheelbarrows has less to do with economics and finance than with the inability of people to realize what was happening to them. Ten notes of one mark each obviously occupy ten times as much space as one note denominated as ten marks, although both will buy ten marks' worth of goods and services. If the prices of goods and services go up tenfold, so that what used to cost one mark now costs ten, but if, at the same time, the Government continues to print as large a proportion of one-mark notes relative to ten-mark notes as before, everyone is clearly going to have to carry ten times as many pieces of paper around with him. This is precisely what happened on these occasions.

If the Government had only cut down on the notes of small denomination and printed more of large denominations, the bulk of paper money to be carried around would have been very much smaller. No wheelbarrows would have been necessary, although, of course, the price inflation would have been just as catastrophic.

But it is here that we find the answer to our question: Who determines the amount of currency and coin in circulation? It is the public—the millions of individuals, business firms, and financial institutions that choose continuously between the use of currency on the one hand and checking accounts on the other. When people want to use more currency, as at Christmas time or when the company treasurer draws the payroll, the amount of currency in circulation goes up and bank deposits tend to go down. After Christmas, when the shopkeepers' cash registers are bulging with currency, they put their excess cash back into the bank and their deposits go up. On payday afternoon or the day after, the workers will also put their excess currency into the bank in exchange for a deposit there.

Thus, the Government prints and mints our currency and coin, but it has no lasting influence on how much of it we keep in circulation and how much of it we deposit in the bank. Of course, this does not mean that the Government has no influence on the supply of money —on the contrary, it has a profound influence on the *total* supply of money in the economy. But that is different from saying that it can determine the relative size of the *parts*. The choice between the use of currency and of checking accounts is made by the public and *only* by the public.

In short, except for the very small amount that the Government issues directly as soldiers' salaries and other payments of that type, all the currency that gets into circulation is withdrawn from bank accounts (just as excess currency in circulation is redeposited in bank accounts). If an employer pays his salaries in currency, he obtains that currency by cashing a check at his local bank. Stores needing currency to make change will draw down their checking accounts to obtain it. At Christmas time, it is a familiar sight to see the long lines of people at the bank, waiting their turn to cash checks for Christmas shopping.

The use of currency, then, is determined by custom and convenience, rather than by any law, regulation, or Government mandate.

On those occasions when we want more currency and draw down our checking accounts, our total amount of money is unchanged: we have more in hand and less in the bank, but the total is neither more nor less than before. And if we obtain our currency by drawing it from the bank, *then the factors that determine the amount of money we have in the bank in the first place will give us the real key to where our money comes from.*

Let us stop here for a moment and survey some of the ground we have already covered. What is to follow has its magical aspects, but it follows logically from the argument that we have built in the preceding pages.

We found, first of all, that money is what we use to buy things. Money is whatever is readily transferable and acceptable to all in payment for goods and services bought and for debts issued and repaid. Anything not readily transferable or whose value is a matter of negotiation rather than instant agreement cannot function as money, because it will lack the general acceptability in payment that is the essential quality of the things we use as money.

We also found and laid great stress on the simple truth that the total supply of money in the country—the number of dollars taking the form of coin, currency, and checking accounts—is independent of the rate at which we spend it. One man's payment is another man's receipt, and vice versa. Money moves from payers to payees, from spenders to receivers, as its ownership shifts continuously back and forth—but the total remains the same.

This leads to two important conclusions, on which all the rest of the story is based.

First, an increase in the supply of money can come only from an increase in the quantity of dollars in currency, coin, or checking accounts. Since we know that an increase in coin and currency comes through withdrawals from checking accounts, it follows that *an increase in the supply of money must originally come about through a rise in checking accounts.*

Second, the only way that somebody can increase his bank account without a transfer from somebody else— that is, the only way one man can have a receipt without another man's making a payment—is if the money he receives comes from some source other than another member of the community. In other words, *some mechanism outside the system is necessary if the supply of money is ever to change at all.*

Could this mechanism be the Government? Conceivably it could be and in the past it has been. Indeed, many of the myths and fears about Government spending flooding the economy with too much money go back to other times and other countries where the government actually did cover its expenses by paying out newly printed currency instead of by borrowing and taxing. But our Government is both legally and morally prohibited from financing its expenditures by printing the money to do it.* The Government is in the same boat as the rest of us—it has to finance its expenditures by obtaining money from somebody else. This it normally does by levying taxation on us or by borrowing the money from us. *But the important point is that the*

---

* Curiously enough, the one exception to this statement occurs when the Government buys gold: it can then print the currency to pay the miner or the nation that sells us the gold. This whole process is analyzed in detail on pp. 113-115.

Government cannot spend money indefinitely without replenishing its bank accounts. In other words, although the Government may spend more than it takes in in taxes, it is unable to spend more than it takes in in taxes *and* borrowings. Thus, a Government surplus or deficit as such has no effect on the total amount of money in the economy, only on its distribution and rate of expenditure.

What is true of the Federal Government is true of each of us: just because one individual or company or government is spending more or less than it takes in, the total supply of money in the economy will not be changed by that deficit or surplus; only the distribution of ownership of money will be changed.

Where, then, can we look for some source of money, someone in a position to pay out money, who is not already a depositor in the banking system? *Indeed, to the banks themselves!* The banks hold our deposits and therefore cannot be depositors *in* themselves. Thus, the man who receives the money that a bank has paid out for some purpose—say, because it has lent him money or bought a security he wanted to sell—will increase his bank balance without having taken money away from any other depositor. Since his larger balance has no offset in a smaller balance elsewhere, the total volume of deposits must be larger than it was before!

This remarkable process is part and parcel of the workaday business of our economy, in which many of us participate to a much greater extent than we realize. It is worth following through in some detail.

CHAPTER V

The Business of Banking

All of this leads to a logical, but nonetheless unexpected, conclusion: it isn't the Government that creates the money we use at all. Rather, the very largest part of the money in our bank accounts today, which we received yesterday and may be spending tomorrow, originally came into being when some commercial bank officer approved a loan to a customer or decided to invest in a marketable security. Of course, this does not mean that we all just borrowed this money or sold securities to a bank to get it; it does mean that, somewhere back along the line, most of the dollars we are now using were created by the lending and investing decisions of commercial bank officers.*

* The use of the adjective "commercial" is extremely important.

And we now begin to look at these proverbially starch-collared, fishy-eyed businessmen from a new viewpoint. These fellows who sit so sternly in judgment on the financial habits of the entire community are actually involved in a much more exciting business than they might be willing to admit. They are, in fact, star players in the drama. We would do well to know more of what they are about.

The history of American banking is littered with the failures of banks that forgot or simply didn't bother to have enough cash on hand to meet the withdrawals demanded by their depositors. While the banker wants to make a profit just as much as the next man, and while the profit in his business comes from lending out and investing the funds his customers deposit with him, he can remain in business only so long as his depositors are confident that he will really give them back their money when they ask for it. Above all, therefore, his skill depends upon his ability to gauge how fast his depositors are likely to be putting money into the bank compared with how fast they will be drawing it out.

The successful banker develops a sensitive feel for these patterns. He knows when his business customers are accumulating inventory and therefore drawing down their cash, and when their sales will exceed their purchases and their balances will build up again. He is

---

Commercial banks are differentiated from savings banks or investment banks or any other kind of bank, in that only commercial banks accept and handle *demand deposits*, the technical term for checking accounts. Commercial banks may do some of the same types of business that other financial institutions do (such as taking savings accounts), but no other institution handles demand deposits. Our attention is focused on the commercial banker, then, because it is checking accounts, in contrast to other types of financial instruments, that we use as money—to pay for the things we buy and to incur and repay debts.

aware that his big corporate customers will be drawing down large sums on dividend payment dates and that all his customers will be busy writing checks at tax time. He knows that currency leaves the bank at Christmas and returns afterward. He watches to see which customers are prospering and tending to carry larger balances as time goes by, while he is also checking continuously to see that his less successful customers do not begin to write checks that their balances will be too small to cover.

Fortunately for the banker, the money a depositor leaves with him is seldom all drawn out immediately: if the depositor were going to draw the money out right after having deposited it, he probably wouldn't have made the deposit in the first place. Some of it may of course be spent almost at once, but some of it will stay with the bank for at least a short period of time and part of it may remain for a long time. Perhaps most important, the banker knows that—so long as people have confidence in his bank—all of his depositors won't ask for all of their money at the same moment.

In short, he bases his decisions on the assumption that he will have to meet withdrawals by some of his depositors all of the time but that he won't have to meet withdrawals by all of his depositors at any one time. Indeed, since some people are putting money in at the same time that others are taking money out, all he really has to pay attention to is the *net* balance between deposits and withdrawals.

No wonder, then, that bankers are characteristically conservative in temperament. This business of always being sure to have money on hand when people ask for it, and of never being quite sure exactly how much or how soon these requests will have to be satisfied, is enough to make anyone want to play a little extra-safe.

But what does the banker do with the money his depositors leave with him?

When a bank begins to gain funds, when the sums being deposited exceed the amounts being withdrawn, the banker will at first simply hold some of that cash idle, earning no interest at all, just to be sure that what seems to be a net inflow does not soon reverse itself and turn into a net outflow. He will, in any case, want to have a pool of cash or of securities he could liquidate readily, to cover him in case money does begin to leave the bank.

The cash that the banker holds to cover the possibility of net withdrawals by his depositors is called a *reserve*. This is a messy bit of nomenclature, because banks also have other kinds of reserves, such as reserves against losses on their loans. But when we are discussing the manner in which a bank meets the possibilities of net withdrawals by its depositors, the word "reserve" always refers to the cash that the bank holds to meet such contingencies.

But just as the banker knows that all of his depositors are not going to ask for all of their money at the same moment, he also can feel reasonably certain that a large or protracted net outflow of funds will be spread over a period of time, not just concentrated into one or two days. He sees no necessity, therefore, to hold more cash than he might need to cover the first few days of a net outflow.

Therefore, in order to supplement his cash reserve, he will carry what he likes to call a "secondary reserve." This means that he will invest some of his available cash in a form that will permit him to turn it back into cash at little risk and on short notice. Very likely he will buy U. S. Treasury obligations that will be maturing in the near future; these will give him back his cash in a short time in any case and, if he needs the cash before maturity, he can readily find a buyer for these securities at a price close to what he paid for them. Such investments will earn some interest—more than he would get if he kept the funds in cash—but will still permit him to take care of a net outflow of funds as it begins to amount up.

Now the banker begins to consider what he might do with the money that he hopes and expects will remain with the bank for an extended period of time. Some of it will consist of funds that depositors keep in their accounts more or less indefinitely as a minimum working balance. A large part of it will consist of dollars whose ownership among the depositors may be shifting but whose total will tend to remain about the same—in other words, dollars that the banker can figure on having available on a long-term basis because he expects one customer's deposit to offset another customer's withdrawal to at least this amount. This is the basic pool of money on which the bank earns enough to cover its operating expenses and show a profit for its stockholders.*

But we must remember the banker's conservative temperament. Although he thinks it *probable* that this money will remain with the bank, he would never be so bold as to think it *certain*. He will, therefore, want to be sure that he puts most of these funds either into se-

---

* Many commercial banks take savings accounts, whose balances also tend to remain for long periods of time. In addition, they take deposits called "time deposits" on which the depositor agrees to leave the money with the bank for some specified period. On both types of deposits, the bank pays interest to the customer. On the other hand, since this money will either remain for a long time or at least for a specified period, the banker needs to hold only a small cash reserve against it and, in fact, can lend or invest it on a relatively long-term basis.

curities that have a good market so that he can sell them on short notice, even at some sacrifice in price, or into loans that the borrower will be paying off within a relatively short period of time. In the past only a small portion of commercial bank assets has consisted of bonds that mature in more than five to ten years or of loans that run beyond one year. Some banks make a fetish of buying only short-term securities (one bank on Wall Street has been accused of having a security portfolio that "matures every five minutes"). In almost all cases, loans that run more than one year usually require monthly or quarterly instalment payments so that at least part of the loan is continuously being paid off.

In deciding how to allocate his resources between marketable securities, on the one hand, and loans, on the other, the banker will consider three factors: liquidity, cost, and demand.

For the reason just cited—namely, that his depositors may surprise him and withdraw more money than he had expected—the banker will always supplement his cash reserve and his secondary reserve with other bonds that may mature in more than thirty or ninety days but that still have a ready market so that they can be sold without difficulty. Indeed, the factor that distinguishes securities from loans in bank operations is that the former have a market where they can be bought from or sold to other investors, whereas the latter must be held until they fall due and are paid off.*

* A hybrid between loans and security investments is known as the "demand loan." This type of loan must be repaid by the borrower on the demand of the bank and is usually secured by marketable securities. Because the collateral is readily marketable, the bank can always be sure of getting its money back by liquidating the securities in case the borrower is unwilling or unable to repay the loan when the bank demands it. On the other hand, many apparently short-term loans are really extended commitments by the bank, as an informal agreement exists between bank and

The banker will also give some consideration to the cost of administering a portfolio of securities as compared with the costs of running a loan and credit department. As the securities the bank is likely to buy are normally the obligations of some first-rate credit risk— the U.S. Government, a state or local government or agency, or a major corporation—little or no investigation is needed before deciding whether the bond is safe to buy. The judgments involved are essentially concerned with interest rate trends and money market patterns.

In a small bank, one officer can run the bond portfolio on a part-time basis, as a sideline in addition to his other duties. Even in a larger bank, the number of people involved in managing the bank's investments is only a small fraction of the personnel required to investigate potential borrowers, follow up and keep track of their financial position, service loans on which repayments or renewals occur frequently, and tend to the unpleasant business of preventing slow or bad loans from turning into a total loss.

Therefore, although the interest rate on securities may some times be as little as half the rate that the bank can earn by lending money directly to its customers, the cost differential will go a long way toward offsetting that difference. However, as the yield on securities tends to fluctuate more widely than the interest rates on loans, the relative attractiveness of the two types of bank assets will vary from one period of time to the next.

Finally, of course, the banker can make loans only to those customers who come around to him and ask to

---

customer to renew the loan when it falls due. Even many instalment loans are renewed for their full original amount before they have been completely paid off.

borrow money. He can't force anyone to borrow, nor will he be willing to lend money to anyone he thinks will be unable to pay the loan off when it falls due. There are times, especially when business conditions are slow, when business firms see no need to expand or to accumulate inventory and are therefore reluctant to borrow and when the credit ratings of many individuals and businesses tend to deteriorate.

In other words, from time to time the banker may want to lend more money than he is able to lend—and this is usually when the interest rate differential makes loans look most attractive, but the opportunities simply aren't there to take advantage of the situation. At such times he will have no alternative but to buy more securities if he wants to keep his interest income up. At other times, of course, the opposite will be the case: when loan demand is strong, bankers will be liquidating or refusing to buy securities so that they can accommodate those customers who are seeking to borrow from them.

The public and the banker sit on opposite sides of the desk or look at each other from opposite sides of the teller's window in a figurative as well as a literal sense. We are all interested in getting money out of the bank, either because we are depositors and will demand our money when we need it, or because we hope to borrow from or sell securities to a bank in order to replenish our own cash resources. The banker wants us to leave as much money as possible with him, even though he lives in a constant state of uncertainty as to our intentions. Furthermore, he never makes a loan without immediately beginning to worry about whether it will be paid off when due, just as he pays close attention to the prices of and market for the securities in which he has invested his bank's cash.

Thus, the banking business is a constant struggle between the necessity to be liquid to meet net withdrawals and the desire to have money lent out and invested so that it will earn interest to show the bank a profit.

But what has all of this to do with the creation of money? A great deal. As we are about to see, it is through this process of lending and investing that the banker functions as midwife in the monetary process.

CHAPTER VI

Bank Credit and Money

The most crucial point in the whole discussion so far is this: that one man's payment is another man's receipt, that one man's deposit comes from another man's withdrawal. From this we can deduce that the total number of dollars in checking accounts can be increased only when one man's deposit is not correspondingly offset by a withdrawal from another man's account.

The only way that this condition can be met is when the funds that one man deposits come, not from another depositor, but from one of the commercial banks themselves. And, in fact, we have just seen that this is precisely what commercial bankers like to do: they want to keep as little cash as possible idle and to invest or lend out the largest part of the funds their depositors put at their disposal.

We can see this more clearly if we go back to our friend the pencil manufacturer, who wants to increase his annual production from 100 million pencils to 110 million. We saw that he will have to finance this increased production. Before he can sell and be paid for the additional 10 million pencils, he himself will have to buy and pay for extra quantities of raw material and labor power.

Perhaps he can obtain the cash he needs by borrowing it from a friend or from an insurance company or a finance company. Possibly he will sell new shares of stock and take new investors into his business. Or, as another possibility, he may liquidate some short-term securities that he had been carrying to provide for just such a contingency. But in each of these cases, the money he receives comes from someone else—the friend, the insurance company, the finance company, the investors, the buyers of the securities he sells. In each of these cases, therefore, his financing results in only a *transfer* of money, not in any increase in the amount of money. He has more now; the others have less.

But suppose, instead, that he goes to one of the officers he knows at the bank where he carries his checking account. He shows the officer his company's latest financial statement and points out to him the rising trend of his sales and the urgent demand for his pencils. He stresses his confidence that the additional production will find buyers and that increased sales receipts will soon bring money in to liquidate the loan. He reminds the officer that he has always carried ample balances with the bank,* so that the bank has had plenty of opportunity to lend out or to invest the money he has left with them.

The bank officer is persuaded by the pencil manufacturer's arguments and approves the loan. He sends an instruction down to the bookkeeping department to increase by, say, $50,000 the amount on their books to the credit of the pencil company. *The company's account is increased just as though a check for $50,000 from some other lender had been deposited in it.*

From the viewpoint of the pencil manufacturer, this transaction is no different from having borrowed the money from a friend or an insurance company. He has to use the same arts of persuasion to obtain the loan. He now has a similar $50,000 worth of perfectly normal and spendable money in his checking account, which he can use to pay his suppliers and employees the amounts that he will owe them.

From the viewpoint of the economy, however, the process is radically different. When the manufacturer borrows from a friend or an insurance company, the money he receives is transferred to him by the lender—he has more money, the lender has less, and the total amount of money is unchanged. But when he borrows from the commercial bank, he has more money but *no one has any less!* His deposit has been increased; nobody's deposit has been reduced. Therefore, he has more money to spend, while no one else has any less. With the punch of a bookkeeping machine, the total amount of purchasing power in the economy has obviously been increased.

. . .

---

* It is a standing joke in business circles that banks lend money only to those who don't need it.

Let us take a somewhat different version of the same process. We shall find that we end up with the same conclusion.

Consider, for example, the possibility that the pencil manufacturer decides to sell $50,000 in Government securities that he has been holding, in preference to borrowing the money to finance his increased production. In order to do this, he is likely to call one of the dealers that make a market in Government securities and to say that he wants to liquidate his securities.

The bond dealer will buy the securities from him. However, these dealers make their money by both buying and selling securities, rather than by just holding them. The dealer will therefore reoffer the pencil manufacturer's securities for sale, hopefully at a profit to himself.

One buyer of these securities may be this same local bank, which has excess cash available to invest. The banker may either have no promising borrowers looking for credit at that moment, or may feel that he had better hold some sort of more liquid asset to cover large net withdrawals that he expects his customers to make in the near future. Accordingly, the banker will buy the $50,000 of securities from the dealer by sending him a check for the proper amount.

Now, we should note the difference between the two steps in this transaction. When the dealer bought the securities from the pencil manufacturer, the familiar sequence of events took place: the pencil manufacturer had $50,000 more in his account after he deposited the dealer's check for that amount, while the dealer had $50,000 less. Money had changed hands, but the total was the same as it had been before. However, when the bank sent its check to pay for the securities it bought from the dealer, the dealer had $50,000 more in his account after he had deposited the bank's check, *but nobody else's checking account had been reduced.* The dealer had replenished the $50,000 he had paid out to the pencil manufacturer, but no one had any less money to spend. Thus, here, too, the supply of money in the economy was increased when a commercial bank came into the picture.

Something seems to be just a little too mysterious, just a little too pat about this sequence of transactions. It is perfectly true, of course, that the pencil manufacturer was able to borrow money from the commercial bank without any other depositor's having to give up the money for him to use—but, after all, the bank will have to give up that money when the manufacturer draws it out to pay his workers and suppliers. Furthermore, when the securities dealer sold the securities to the bank, he got back the $50,000 he had paid out to the pencil manufacturer without receiving the money from any other depositor, but the bank still had to turn over the $50,000 to the dealer (or, to be precise, to the bank in which the dealer deposited the check for $50,000).

Therefore, while we must admit that in both instances the amount of money in checking accounts went up without anybody's account going down, the fact remains that the bank is still going to be out $50,000, whether it lent the money to the pencil manufacturer or was the ultimate buyer of the securities he had to sell.

Indeed, if we were to visit the commercial banker and tell him that he has a wonderful deal because he can create money out of nothing—really, with the stroke of a pen—he would be profoundly shocked and would tell us that we don't know what we are talking about.

He would deny any connection with such a printing press operation and would insist that he is no more capable of creating money than a savings bank or an insurance company or any individual he can think of.

In fact, whether he is the fishy-eyed type or the more friendly model, the banker would point out that he cannot even lend or invest all the cash that he has, because he must always have enough on hand to meet the net withdrawals that his depositors are likely to make. No matter how we cross-examine him on this point, he is sure to be adamant about it. He would stress that his bank loses cash when he has to pay for the securities he buys. He would point out, too, that borrowers usually draw out the proceeds of loans in short order, for no one borrows money and pays interest on it for the sheer joy of seeing a larger bank balance. They soon start writing checks and, when they do, his bank will be losing cash to the banks in which these checks are ultimately deposited.

Then has our analysis up to this point been incorrect? Can we really say that new money is created when commercial banks make loans or buy securities just because demand deposits go up as a result? Are those new deposits money or aren't they? If the banker loses cash when he lends or invests, how then can he be creating money?

No, the analysis is *not* incorrect. New money *is* created in response to credit expansion by commercial banks. Although it is perfectly true that the bank will lose cash when it lends and invests, the bank has nevertheless created money. No matter how adamant the banker may be, he *is* a magician of sorts.

What is the solution to the paradox?

Remember that money is what we use to buy things

with, and surely this includes the balances in our check-ing accounts. This point is the real key to the mystery.

When the security dealer sold the U.S. Treasury se-curities to the bank and deposited the bank's check in his account, that additional balance was just as avail-able for him to spend as every other dollar that he had in his account or that all other depositors in the coun-try had in their accounts. He has more to spend than he had before; no other depositor has any less. Similarly, when the pencil manufacturer borrowed the money from the bank, the additional dollars the bank officer authorized him to draw were just as spendable, just as acceptable, as all the other dollars in his and all other checking accounts. He, too, has more to spend; no other depositor has any less.

But what about the cash that the bank had to give up when it bought the securities or when the pencil manu-facturer began to draw down the proceeds of the loan? Isn't that an offset to the additional spending power that the security dealer or the pencil manufacturer have available to them?

To answer this question, let us see what happened to this cash that the bank apparently had to part with. Where did it go? When the bank bought securities, the dealer deposited the bank's check in his own account, and his bank collected the $50,000 from the bank that bought the securities.* When the loan was made to the pencil manufacturer and he drew checks in favor of his workers and suppliers, those checks were deposited in their banks, which in turn collected the money from the bank that had made the loan to the pencil manu-facturer. In other words, *the $50,000 that left one*

---

* The mechanism by which one bank turns funds over to an-other in payment of its depositors withdrawals is explained below on pp. 63-64.

bank ended up by being deposited in other banks in the system.

This is the key to the whole process: *every withdrawal from one checking account is offset by a deposit in another.** The reason for this, of course, is simply that checking accounts are the most convenient means for holding money and for transferring it to others, so that when we receive payments from people who owe us money for one reason or another, the most logical thing to do with those receipts is to deposit them in our own checking accounts. Thus, while one bank can in fact lose cash when its depositors are withdrawing funds, that cash remains within the banking *system* because it ends up in the possession of some other bank.

Therefore, our adamant banker is both right and wrong. He is absolutely correct in saying that he can neither lend nor invest more than he has available in cash and that, in fact, he can actually lend and invest *less* because he has to be alert to his depositors' demands for withdrawals. Thus, he has no sense at all of creating money out of thin air—how can he be creating money where none was there before? But he is wrong, nevertheless, if he denies that he is in fact creating money: his payments to borrowers or to investors from whom he buys securities do increase their spending power without reducing anyone else's, and, while his own bank will lose cash, the banking system does not. *All banks together are not limited by cash on hand. One bank's loss is another bank's gain.*

Our banker is now giving ground, but he is still not completely convinced. He admits that new deposits are

---

* This is an unavoidable oversimplification that is essential at this point for our understanding of the process. Later we shall drop this assumption and find that factors such as net currency withdrawals, gold outflows, and Federal Reserve operations can result in withdrawals without offsetting deposits.

created when he pays out the proceeds of a loan or a security purchase. He agrees that no old deposits are reduced at the same time, so that on balance the spending power of the public has indeed been increased. He concedes that the commercial banks as a group lose no cash as a result of this process, since one bank's loss is another bank's gain. But why are the commercial banks then unique in the process of money creation? What about savings banks? What about individuals? Can they then create money too?

No, they cannot. Suppose you borrow some money from a savings bank—say, to finance the purchase of a new home. How does the savings bank pay out to you the proceeds of that loan? It pays by issuing a check, just as the commercial bank might pay it. *But the check that the savings bank draws is on its own checking account in a commercial bank!* When you deposit that check in your own account, it will clear through the commercial banking system and end up reducing the balance held by the savings bank. Your checking account will be up, the savings bank's will be down—no change in total spending power. The savings bank is just like any other depositor in the system, and the savings bank system has lost cash.

But why does the savings bank have to carry a checking account? Why must it be a depositor in the commercial banking system? Wherein is it different from the commercial banks?

The answer is simply that we do use checking accounts as money and do not use savings accounts. The money that we withdraw from the savings bank is deposited in our checking account rather than in another savings account, because it is *spendable* money when it is in a checking account; it is a nontransferable, only partly liquid asset when it is in a savings account. Thus, when a savings bank makes a payment, it must draw down its checking account at a commercial bank and nothing more than a *transfer* of money occurs.

In short, we do not use savings accounts or cash values of life insurance policies as money—as a means of exchange to pay for things we buy or to pay off debts incurred. If we did, the same process would apply to them that applies to commercial banks.

For example, *if* we were in the habit of paying for things simply by presenting our savings bank passbook, and *if* the seller put the proceeds into his savings account, *then* we would be using savings accounts as money. Then when we borrowed money from a savings bank or when a savings bank bought some securities that we were selling, we would be willing to take the proceeds in the form of an increase in our savings accounts—for we would be able to spend the proceeds in that form. Then the savings bank system would never lose cash and would, in effect, be creating money. But, since we do *not* pay for things with savings accounts, we would normally refuse to take the proceeds of a loan or a security sale in the form of an increased savings deposit. What we do want is either currency or an increase in our checking account, because only then can we transfer the proceeds—that is spend the money —for whatever purpose prompted us to borrow or to liquidate some asset in the first place.

Nor do we do business by making payments or accepting payments in the form of cash values of life insurance. To do so would mean, for example, that the dealer who sold us a new car would be willing to have $3000 transferred to the cash value of his life insurance policy from the cash value of the buyer's insurance policy. And, then, if transfers of life insurance cash values

were readily acceptable forms of payment, we would
also be willing to take the proceeds of money borrowed
from an insurance company as an increase in our life
insurance cash value—for we could then transfer that
cash value to some one else and thereby be able to
spend those proceeds. But we don't do business that
way either.

Finally, consider the case of John Jones. If checks
written on his account by John Jones were acceptable
all over the United States as payment for goods and
services sold and for debts incurred—even by people
who never heard of John Jones—then John Jones could
write an infinite number of checks on his account. He
would, in effect, be printing currency, for no one would
ever come to him and ask him to make good. Then he
could lend out or invest all the money he wanted simply by writing additional checks; the checks would pass
continuously from hand to hand, because they would
be acceptable to all, and so John Jones would be creating money. But we don't do business this way either.

*The unique characteristic of the commercial banks
is that, essentially, no one asks them to "make good."*
Money paid out by one commercial bank is redeposited in another commercial bank, because it retains its
spendable form that way. Whatever we want to call
them—checking accounts, demand deposits, claims on
the commercial banking system—these deposits serve
as a substitute for currency or coin as a means of payment. There isn't anything else that we use in this
particular fashion.

It is also important to remember that no law requires us to do business in this manner. Only custom,
custom based on convenience. Indeed, the laws and
regulations that apply to the commercial banking system have been developed to make this process work as

smoothly as possible, but the process came first and the laws and regulations afterward. If some other type of asset or claim—savings accounts, insurance policies, or even diamond necklaces—were as convenient a form of payment as checking accounts, that is what we would use and our laws and regulations would have to be adjusted accordingly.

This brings up for closer examination the observation that we made earlier: the largest part of the money we use is created, not by the Government, but by the lending and investing decisions of individual commercial bank officers.

The intriguing aspect of this process is that the banker doesn't make loans or buy securities because he wants to create money—he gives this little or no thought. Rather, his attention is simply directed to how much of his available cash resources he can lend or invest and still have enough on hand to cover his depositors' demands for withdrawals—a very limited and parochial view of a process with a profound impact on the level of employment, production, and prices in the national economy.

Yet, here, for example, is what the total figures (in billions of dollars) looked like for the 13,500 commercial banks in the United States at the end of 1963 compared with the end of 1962:

	1963	1962	Net change
Cash assets	50.9	54.0	Down 3.1
Loans and investments	253.3	235.8	Up 17.5
Deposits*	274.9	262.1	Up 12.8

* The difference between deposits, on the one hand, and cash and earning assets, on the other, is accounted for primarily by the capital accounts of the banks.

Note that the banks lent out and purchased securities to the tune of more than 17 billion dollars during 1963, but that their cash assets went down by only 3 billion dollars. What happened, in effect, was that the people who borrowed from the banks or who sold securities the banks bought took almost all that money in the form of additional deposits in commercial banks* instead of in some other form that would have required them to draw the money out of the commercial banking system.

This leads to an even more asymmetrical view of things by the individual banker, on the one hand, and our view of the system as a whole, on the other. If the individual banker is to make loans and buy securities, his customers must first make deposits in his bank so that he has the cash available to lend or invest. But if money is to be circulating around so that his customers can make deposits in the first place, the banking system must be making loans and buying securities! In the individual bank, the loans and investments follow from the deposits; in the system as a whole, the deposits are created by the loans and investments.

Again, all of this is true because of our custom of using checking accounts as money, of depositing in our checking accounts the money we receive from others. Basic to the whole process is the necessity that one man's withdrawal end up as another man's deposit. Since money withdrawn from one man's savings account or life insurance policy is not automatically redeposited in another savings account or life insurance policy, the savings banks and insurance companies (and all other

---

* Some of the proceeds of the loans and investments ended up in commercial bank time deposits rather than in checking accounts. This complication is discussed in detail below. See Chapter XIV.

individuals, institutions, and corporations) must have money flowing in before they can lend it out or invest it. But so long as money leaving one commercial bank is redeposited in another, *the commercial banking system does not need fresh money coming in before loans and investments can be increased.*

But since this process goes on with each individual commercial bank looking out for its own self-interest, and since each bank wants to lend out and invest just as much as it can based on its judgment as to the probable demands of its depositors for withdrawals, some sort of control over this process is necessary.

For example, has the public any assurance that the banks will, in fact, keep enough cash on hand to cover their withdrawals? What does the bank do when it has to meet withdrawals but the moment is a bad one for selling securities or saying no to credit-worthy borrowers? What happens when one man's withdrawal is *not* offset by another man's deposit and when, as a result, not just one or two, but many banks are trying to sell securities to raise cash? If everyone is trying to sell, who will buy? And how can we be certain that the rate at which banks are creating new money is appropriate to the level of business activity in the national economy —neither so slow that expenditures are excessively difficult to finance nor so rapid that inflation can result? In short, how do things work out when we drop our simplifying assumption that money *never* leaves or enters the commercial banking system?

All of these questions have spelled trouble for the American economy at one time or another in our history. Some of them still do. But at least we have developed a mechanism that attempts to deal with problems of this type—sometimes with more success, sometimes with less. That mechanism is known as the Federal Reserve System. The mechanics of that System are analyzed in Part Three and its performance is assessed in Part Four.

Part Three

THE CONTROL
OF MONEY

CHAPTER VII

The Federal Reserve
System

The Federal Reserve System was established by Congress in 1913, following the banking crisis of 1907. All of the questions raised at the end of Chapter VI had applied with a vengeance to the events of 1907, and this was only the most intense of a long sequence of similar crises. It was hoped that the Federal Reserve System would prevent a repetition of such disasters. Although unable to stem the cataclysmic worldwide breakdown of the early 1930's, the Federal Reserve has met most of the challenges for which its framers originally designed it. To the extent that controversy surrounds the Federal Reserve, this is a result of efforts to meet objectives beyond those set forth in 1913.

The structure of the Federal Reserve System is an outstanding example of American political genius, for it neatly combines local and national authorities, at the same time blending public and private responsibility.

The country has been divided into twelve Federal Reserve Districts, each district having a Federal Reserve Bank in its major financial center (although several of the banks have one or more branches throughout the District). In addition to the twelve banks, a Board of Governors sits in Washington as the major policy-making body.

Decisions for each of the twelve banks are made by a nine-member Board of Directors, divided into three groups of three men each. The three Class A Directors are all bankers elected by the district's commercial banks that have joined the Federal Reserve System. The three Class B Directors are also elected by the local commercial banks, but are businessmen from the district who are not bankers. Finally, the three Class C Directors, although residents of the district, are appointed by the Board of Governors in Washington. These Class C Directors are a varied group of business and professional men—even college professors have occasionally served as Class C Directors.

The Board of Governors consists of seven men, appointed by the President of the United States, with the consent of the Senate, for fourteen-year terms.*

---

* Legislation is pending to make the Chairman's term run for only four years, to coincide with the term of office of the President of the United States.

The purpose of these long appointments is to make the Board relatively independent of political pressures, although the system of appointment by the President nevertheless keeps the Board from being completely unresponsive to popular sentiment.

Although the ultimate seat of responsibility is in the Board of Governors, certain decisions are made at the initiative of the Federal Reserve Banks (subject to approval by the Board in Washington) and others are made by a committee that consists of the seven members of the Board and the Presidents of five of the banks. In other words, local and national interests and public and business viewpoints intertwine at almost all points in the policy-making process of the monetary authorities.

Finally, who belongs to the Federal Reserve System and why? Some 6000 banks—a little less than half of the commercial banks in the nation—have joined the System and are known as "member banks." Although a minority of the banks in the country, these banks nevertheless contain more than two thirds of total commercial bank deposits.

Membership in the System stipulates certain restrictions as to lending and investing policies. The banks are regularly examined by officials of the Federal Reserve Banks to make certain that the quality of their loans and investments meets the required standards. Equally important, and especially appropriate from our viewpoint here, member banks must carry a minimum amount of cash reserves in relation to their outstanding deposits, this minimum being set from time to time by the Board of Governors in Washington.

Why should a bank submit to these restrictions? There are two major incentives for membership.*

* About three quarters of the member banks are banks with

First, prestige attaches to it: it implies that a member bank is a safer place in which to deposit money, precisely because the bank has submitted to the restrictions and rules on which the Reserve authorities insist. Thus, membership helps attract deposits. Second, member banks have the privilege of borrowing from the Federal Reserve Banks when they have insufficient cash to cover their depositors' withdrawals—a privilege that gives our whole banking system much more flexibility than it would otherwise have.

The focal point of all of this machinery—the twelve Federal Reserve Banks, the Board of Governors, the rules and regulations of membership—is the supply of member bank cash reserves relative to the volume of deposits outstanding in the banks. It is this relationship that each banker must consider in deciding whether to make additional loans or to let some loans run off without replacing them, and whether to purchase or sell securities for the bond portfolio.

Thus, through control of the supply of member bank reserves, the Federal Reserve authorities attempt to influence member banks to increase or decrease their credit operations and, thereby, to expand or contract the quantity of money—the purchasing power in checking accounts. In short, whereas the focal point of Federal Reserve operations is the supply of member bank reserves, the ultimate object of their activities is to regulate the quantity of money.

There is nothing complicated about the mechanics

---

national rather than state charters. As all national banks are required to belong to the Federal Reserve System, they have no choice in the matter unless they wish to shift to a state charter. However, many of the largest and most important banks in New York and Chicago, the nation's major financial centers, are state-chartered but belong to the Federal Reserve nevertheless.

of Federal Reserve operations. In fact, we have only one thing to keep in mind: the Reserve Banks are bankers' banks—that is, they function in relation to the member banks in precisely the same way that the commercial banks function in relation to the public. Below are some important illustrations of this relationship.

As the public holds most of its ready money in the form of deposits in commercial banks, so the commercial banks hold most of their cash resources in the form of deposits at the Federal Reserve Banks.

As the commercial banks provide a convenient means for an individual or business firm to make payments by transferring funds to another individual or business firm through the use of checking accounts— that is, through simple bookkeeping procedures—so the Federal Reserve System provides a convenient way for one bank to transfer funds to another bank through bookkeeping procedures rather than through any physical transfer of cash.

As the public deposits its excess currency holdings in checking accounts at commercial banks, where it is more conveniently spendable, and as the public also replenishes its supply of currency by withdrawals from checking accounts, so commercial banks will draw down their accounts at the Federal Reserve Banks when they need additional amounts of currency to satisfy the public. And so, also, the commercial banks will redeposit at the Federal Reserve excess currency that accumulates in their vaults.

Finally, as a consequence of these other considerations, the granting of loans by the Federal Reserve Banks and their purchases of securities will result in an increase in member bank deposits at the Reserve banks, for the same reasons that commercial bank lending and

investing will cause the volume of checking account
money to increase.

Let us consider each of these similarities in turn.

In the early days of banking, each bank kept its
cash reserve in the form of actual currency or coin or
gold bullion. However, when one bank was losing deposits to other banks—that is, when withdrawals exceeded new deposits—the physical transfer of cash from
bank to bank in this form was most inconvenient. This
led many banks, particularly banks outside the money
market centers, to deposit any excess currency and coin
in a checking account with another bank, usually located in a money market center, such as New York or
Chicago. This centralized the physical cash reserves of
the banking system in these financial centers, where
the larger banks served as banks both to the public
and to their correspondents throughout the country.

The bankers' banks made it possible for some bank
in the interior of the country to lose cash as a result of
an excess of withdrawals, without having to make any
physical transfers of funds. Banks losing cash to other
banks simply had their accounts reduced on the books
of their big-city depository, while banks gaining funds
had their accounts increased. This system still persists
in many instances, because of the convenience it provides.

When the Federal Reserve System was established,
this business of banks' carrying their cash reserves in
the form of deposits at other banks was largely centralized in the Federal Reserve Banks. The attraction
of carrying the cash reserve at a Reserve Bank instead
of another commercial bank is rooted in the legal obligations of Federal Reserve membership: member banks
are required to hold a stipulated minimum of cash re-

serves in relation to the volume of their outstanding deposits—and the only cash reserve that satisfies this legal requirement is the member bank's balance at the Federal Reserve Bank (plus currency and coin the bank has in its vaults). Thus, although banks are still free to carry balances with correspondent banks, these correspondent balances do not count as part of the legal reserve that a member bank is required to maintain. This means that the largest part of member bank cash is kept in the form of deposits at the Federal Reserve Banks.

In addition to the legal paraphernalia that has resulted in these arrangements, they have a practical attraction as well. The public carries most of its cash in the form of deposits at commercial banks because they provide such a convenient form of transferring funds in payment for goods purchased or debts incurred. Similarly, the use of Federal Reserve accounts is a great convenience for commercial banks, who are always busy transferring funds back and forth among themselves.

Take, for example, the cash of John Jones, who lives in Albany and wants to send $7.50 to New York City for a subscription to a magazine called *Tide*. Mr. Jones could of course send currency through the mail or buy a money order at the postoffice. However, he finds it much more convenient simply to write a check on the Albany National Bank in the amount of $7.50 and payable "to the order of" *Tide Magazine*. Note that when *Tide Magazine* receives the check, Mr. Jones still has that $7.50 in his account in Albany, and, in fact, *Tide* cannot spend the money until one of its officers has deposited the check in the magazine's account at its New York bank.

Tide deposits Mr. Jones's check in its account at the New York State Bank. The bookkeeper at New York

State Bank increases the *Tide* account by $7.50, but *Tide still* can't spend that money—neither *Tide* nor *Tide*'s bank knows for sure at this moment whether Mr. Jones will really have $7.50 in his account when the check gets back to Albany. The bookkeeper therefore notes that the $7.50 will remain "uncollected"—that is, unavailable for *Tide* to withdraw—for five days; by that time, they will have had time to hear from Albany if Mr. Jones had sufficient funds to cover his check.

The interesting aspect of this process is that the commercial banks use the Federal Reserve in precisely the same way that the public uses the commercial banks. *Tide* naturally deposited Mr. Jones's check in its checking account at its local bank, letting the bank take care of collecting the $7.50 and, subsequently, paying out the $7.50 when *Tide* will draw out the money to spend for its own purposes. New York State Bank does exactly the same thing with the Federal Reserve Bank of New York: it deposits Mr. Jones's check in its account at the Federal Reserve. The Federal Reserve bookkeeper now notes that New York State Bank's balance will be increased by $7.50 as soon as they are certain that the check is "good."

Since both the Albany National Bank and the New York State Bank are depositors at the Federal Reserve, the transfer of funds from Albany to New York is simple enough. The New York bank's account has already been increased; the Albany bank's account is now reduced by $7.50 and the check is sent on to the Albany National Bank for processing there.*

* In the case where the two commercial banks are in different districts, the principles involved are the same, although the details vary slightly. The magazine would deposit its check in its local bank in the same way, and the local bank would in turn deposit the check in the Federal Reserve Bank of New York. The Federal Reserve Bank of New York would send the check in turn to the

The Albany National now receives the check, notes the reduction in its cash balance at the Federal Reserve, and accordingly reduces Mr. Jones's balance on their books. The final step is a repetition of this: as the Albany National received the check from the Federal Reserve Bank and noted the reduction in its account there, so Mr. Jones will receive his check back at the end of the month from Albany National and confirm that his account has been decreased.

In addition to the clear symmetry between the relationship of public depositor and commercial bank on the one hand and commercial bank and Federal Reserve Bank on the other, one other point is worth stressing here. The process we have just seen shows how easily and conveniently money can be transferred from one person to another and from one part of the country to another purely through punching keys on bookkeeping machines. While the check travels around, no actual physical transfer of cash is involved. We may never see or feel the trillions of dollars that change hands in the United States in the course of a year, but, nevertheless, they travel on over four billion checks with far greater speed, convenience, and safety than if all payments had to be made in gold or silver coin or in paper money.

As we saw some time back, incidentally, we obtain the currency and coin we need by withdrawing it from checking accounts in commercial banks—that is, by "cashing" checks. When we find we have more currency and coin than we need, as happens to shop-

---

Federal Reserve Bank in the district in which Mr. Jones's bank is located—say, the Federal Reserve Bank of Chicago. The gain in funds by the New York Reserve Bank and the loss of funds by the Chicago Reserve Bank is accounted for on the books of the Interdistrict Settlement Fund operated by the Board of Governors in Washington.

keepers when the money flows in to them during the Christmas season, they will replenish their checking accounts by depositing that excess currency in their bank accounts.

But where do the banks obtain the currency that we withdraw, and what do they do with the excess currency that we redeposit and which accumulates in their vaults? They withdraw it, of course, from the Federal Reserve Banks, which in turn reduce the member bank deposit accounts by the corresponding amount. (Thus, in effect, the commercial banks also "cash" checks.) Subsequently, when the commercial banks find that the quantity of currency in their vaults exceeds the working balance they need to take care of their customers' requests, they will ship the excess currency back to the Federal Reserve Bank and replenish their deposit accounts there as a result. Thus, as the commercial banks are to the public, so the Federal Reserve Banks are a source of currency for the commercial banks on the one hand, and a depository for their excess currency supplies on the other.

The Federal Reserve Banks provide one further service function that will have considerable interest for us later on. The United States Treasury uses the Federal Reserve Banks as its main depository and all checks drawn by the Treasury to cover Federal Government outlays are drawn on the Treasury accounts at the Federal Reserve Banks.

The Treasury does carry accounts with commercial banks under certain limited circumstances. For example, if the Treasury issues some new bonds or other securities to borrow money, the commercial banks may be permitted to buy these securities and pay for them simply by increasing the balance on their books to the credit of the Treasury. These accounts, which are known as Tax and Loan Accounts, are also increased when business depositors in commercial banks want to remit withholding and Social Security taxes of their employees. These sums are placed immediately to the credit of the Treasury in the Tax and Loan Account.

The Treasury draws no checks against these accounts, however. As the balances in the accounts build up, the Treasury will issue a "call" on part of the balance to its credit. In response to the call, the balances of the commercial banks at the Federal Reserve Banks will be reduced and the balance of the Treasury at the Federal Reserve will be increased; the commercial banks will, of course, also reduce the Treasury balance on their books at the same time.

But this is not the only type of transaction that increases the Treasury's balance at the Federal Reserve and reduces member bank reserve accounts at the same time. Much money is paid directly to the Treasury rather than passing through the Tax and Loan Accounts—for example, checks drawn by depositors in commercial banks to pay for income and excise taxes or to pay for new Treasury securities purchased may be deposited immediately by the Treasury in its accounts at the Federal Reserve Banks.

Take the case of Mr. Jones, who draws a check on the New York State Bank for $1000 to pay his income tax. The Treasury will deposit that check in the Federal Reserve Bank of New York. The Federal Reserve Bank will increase the Treasury's account by $1000 and reduce the New York State Bank's balance on its books by $1000, after which the New York State Bank will also reduce Mr. Jones's balance by $1000. *But note that this is a case where one bank's loss is not another bank's gain:* the money withdrawn from New York State

Bank did *not* reappear as a deposit in some other commercial bank. The loss of reserves by New York State Bank was a loss for the system *as a whole*. Nor can we say that the funds were gained by the Federal Reserve Bank, for the Federal Reserve Bank gained nothing—it merely transferred the credit balance of $1000 on its books from the account of New York State Bank to the account of the Treasury.

But, of course, the opposite is also true when the Treasury is paying out money faster than it is depositing the receipts of taxes or new borrowings. While the Treasury will take in much more than it is paying out during tax time, and particularly during the middle of April, disbursements tend to exceed receipts during much of the remainder of the year.

Suppose, for example, the Treasury draws a check for $100 to Mr. Jones for his monthly old age pension. He will deposit that check in the New York State Bank, which will in turn deposit the check at the Federal Reserve Bank of New York. The Federal Reserve will increase the New York State Bank's account on its books by $100 and reduce the Treasury's balance by $100. Here the New York State Bank has gained and no other bank has lost—a net gain for the banking system as a whole. The Federal Reserve Bank has gained nothing through the $100 deposit made there by the New York State Bank, for the increase in that bank's account is offset by the reduction in the Treasury's account.

The point of all this is that we have now found one case (and we shall subsequently find others) in which the commercial banking system as a whole can gain or lose reserves. In such cases, the increase or decrease in the cash resources of one bank is not offset by decreases or increases in the cash resources of some other bank.

Just as payments by commercial banks to the public are the mechanism that increases one man's holding of money without decreasing another man's, so payments in and out of the Federal Reserve Banks can change one bank's reserve balance without offsetting changes in another's.

These are the mechanics of the relationship between the Federal Reserve Banks and the member banks. These are also the service functions that the Reserve Banks provide for their members. But the real importance of the Federal Reserve System is the structure that employs these mechanics to raise or lower the reserve balances of the member banks, and, through them, the quantity of money in the economy.

CHAPTER VIII

Federal Reserve Tools
of Control

Although the Federal Reserve authorities can do little or nothing to influence the *rate* at which money is spent, they do exercise significant control over the *quantity of money available* to be spent. They do this, in large part, by causing member bank reserve balances to go up or down and thereby enlarging or reducing the lending and investing capacity of the commercial banking system. But each individual commercial banker watches more than just the size of his cash assets; he also watches how they move in relation to the claims that his depositors may make upon him. Thus, the relationship between cash reserves and deposit liabilities is the principal point at which Federal Reserve policy attempts to regulate the quantity of money in the economy.

In order to observe how the tools of Federal Reserve policy actually operate in practice, let us backtrack for a moment and consider what the situation would be like if no Federal Reserve existed.

Take the case of a bank that has been making loans and investing money at a rapid rate so that its cash resources are being depleted as the borrowers withdraw the proceeds of the loans and as the sellers of the securities bought by the bank have to be paid. The drain on cash may, in fact, reach the point where reserves reach a dangerously low level and the officers of the bank fear that they will have insufficient cash to cover withdrawals that their depositors are expected to make.*

What can the bank do about this situation? Three alternatives are available:

First, the bank can reverse its policy of buying securities and can, instead, start selling securities, so that cash will flow back in rather than going out.

Second, the bank can slow the rate at which it approves new loans, thereby staunching the drain on its cash reserves.

Third, the bank might find some other bank with excess reserves that our bank could borrow, until such time as its depositors resume putting more money in the bank than they are taking out.†

---

* The consequences would of course be the same for a bank with no change in its loans and investments but where depositors are taking out more than they are putting in.

† Lending reserves for brief periods of time back and forth among banks is a daily activity that runs into many millions of dollars. In fact, a market exists in which those banks with excess reserves sell reserves at a price to banks that are short. This is

Now, these three types of adjustments are made by many banks every day of the week. In most instances, they cause no problem at all, for while some banks are short on cash and have to take steps of this type, other banks will have excess cash reserves and will find no difficulty in transferring to banks that need it the cash they require. Our bank, after all, ran short of cash because its depositors were withdrawing money faster than they were depositing it—but, presumably, the money they were spending is redeposited in some other bank. That bank will now have the excess cash needed to restore our bank's liquidity.

Suppose, however, that the other commercial banks find themselves in the same boat. Perhaps they, too, have been aggressive about lending money out and making investments, or perhaps they have also been losing funds through depositors' withdrawals that somehow failed to reappear in the system. Under these conditions, serious trouble can develop. It did, in fact, develop frequently before the establishment of the Federal Reserve System.

Suppose our bank attempts to restore its cash position by selling securities. The buyer of the securities will, of course, pay the bank with a check drawn on his own bank. As that check moves through the collection process, the buyer's bank will lose reserves to the bank that sold the securities. But now the second bank will have to restore its cash position. It will also begin to sell securities—and will thus drain cash away from a third bank. And so on and so on, with the result that suddenly we have only sellers of securities and no buyers.

---

known as the market for Federal funds. The price of Federal funds varies with demand and supply, but never goes above the rate of interest on reserves borrowed directly from the Federal Reserve Banks.

As panic develops in the security markets, depositors become frightened that their banks will have insufficient cash to make good their withdrawals, and "runs" begin in which depositors rush to convert their checking accounts into currency.

Under these circumstances, checking accounts cease to be an acceptable means of payment and only currency and coin will do the job.

The same end result comes of a decision throughout the banking system to slow down on new loans and to insist on full repayment rather than renewals of old loans. Borrowers must, of course, have money on deposit in the bank if they are to pay off their loans. That means that borrowers must be depositing more money than they are withdrawing; it also means that they are no longer paying money out and fattening the checking accounts of those business firms where they had been spending borrowed money. But if everyone wants to take money in and no one wants to pay it out, no money will change hands and no one will be able to establish the position of liquidity he needs. In such circumstances, businesses, banks, and security markets are all thrown into a panic.

The third alternative we mentioned was that one bank short on cash reserves might borrow the cash it needed from another bank with excess reserves. However, this is obviously impossible if all banks are short on cash—they can't all be borrowers and still have cash to lend out.

Of course, we can also visualize the opposite situation, in which the reserves of the banks are so ample that they can go on making loans and purchasing securities—and thereby creating new purchasing power in the economy—for a long time before they begin to run short. This may be fine if business is slack and men are unemployed; then the existence of plenty of money in the economy will make a rising level of output easy to finance and, in fact, large holdings of cash may induce individuals and business firms to go out and buy goods and services. But if business is booming, the excess liquidity resulting from a rapid expansion in commercial bank credit is likely to stoke the fires of inflation, leading to speculation and distortions in the boom that will ultimately bring about an economic crash.

If the function of the Federal Reserve System can be summarized succinctly, we can say that it is to prevent both the occasion in which everyone is a seller and no one a buyer (the money panic just described) and also to prevent the occasion in which everyone is a buyer and no one a seller (which is what happens in an inflation). But as we shall see in Part Five, the Reserve authorities have had a difficult time navigating the swirling and treacherous narrows between the Scylla of too little bank credit and the Charybdis of too much.

Let us see first, however, how the introduction of the Federal Reserve to the monetary system can help to avoid the type of wholesale liquidation and panic that result from a general shortage of cash reserves among the commercial banks.

One way that a commercial bank can replenish its reserves is by selling securities, but, as we saw, this only drains cash away from other banks in which the buyers of the securities maintain their accounts. The problem of overcoming a shortage of cash is simply transferred from the first bank to the others; since one bank's gain is another bank's loss, the total quantity of reserves available to the banking system has remained unchanged.

Suppose, however, that the securities offered for sale by the bank short on reserves are bought, not by a depositor in another commercial bank, but by the Federal Reserve Banks. This can happen if the Reserve Banks are willing to outbid other buyers and thereby run up the prices of the securities. Now we have a *deus ex machina*. Just as before, the selling bank receives a check in payment for the securities it sold. Just as before, it deposits that check in its Federal Reserve account. Just as before, its cash position is restored to the desired level. What is different—and crucially so—is that no other bank in the system has lost any reserves; one bank's gain is *not* offset by another bank's loss. In effect, the Federal Reserve Banks, by buying the securities, have paid to the selling bank the additional reserves it needed, so that no other bank had to lose reserves to accommodate the situation.

The Federal Reserve, as we have noted, pays for the securities by issuing a cashier's check drawn on itself. Does the Federal Reserve lose cash as a result of this transaction? The Federal Reserve Banks no more lose cash when they buy securities than the commercial banking *system* loses cash in similar transactions. The commercial banks as a group lose no cash because the checks they write to pay for the securities they buy are redeposited by sellers in their accounts in commercial banks. Similarly, the checks that the Reserve Banks write to pay for the securities they buy are deposited back in the Federal Reserve Banks by the banks that are gaining the reserves.*

* If the Federal Reserve Banks happen to buy securities when the seller is a depositor in the commercial banking system rather

The reasons for this similarity relate to what we have seen already. Checks issued by commercial banks to pay for the securities they buy are redeposited by the sellers in other commercial banks, thereby keeping cash in the system instead of drawing it out, because it is so convenient for us to keep our money in the form of checking accounts in commercial banks. Checks issued by the Federal Reserve Banks to pay for the securities they buy are redeposited by the commercial banks in the Federal Reserve Banks because it is so convenient for commercial banks to hold their cash reserves in the form of accounts at the Federal Reserve Banks—these balances facilitate interbank transfers and also meet the need for legal reserves to be held against their deposits.

This is more than a matter of mechanics, however. By providing the commercial banks with additional reserves, the Federal Reserve either prevents a shortage of reserves from spreading throughout the system, thereby forcing a reduction in the supply of money as other banks are impelled to sell securities and retract loans, or it actually encourages an increase in the supply of money by creating additional reserves for the commercial banks.* Furthermore, by coming into the bond markets as an additional (and substantial) buyer,

---

than a commercial bank itself, the process is essentially the same. The seller deposits the check he receives from the Federal Reserve into his checking account; his bank, as with any other check, deposits this check in its Federal Reserve account. The only difference here is that deposits as well as reserves have increased in the commercial bank—part of the expansion in the money supply potentially available from the increase in bank reserves has, in effect, already taken place.

* Some Federal Reserve open market operations are designed to *offset* fortuitous or seasonal changes in member bank reserves, and thus to hold them steady. Others are designed to *change* the level of member bank reserves, and thus to influence commercial bank credit policies. This distinction is discussed more fully below.

the Federal Reserve pushes bond prices to a higher level than they would otherwise have reached. This is the same thing as saying that bond *yields* move lower.

In short, then, purchases of securities by the Federal Reserve Banks make the financing of a business expansion both easier and less expensive; banks are more willing to provide new credits, and interest rates are lower than they would have been without Federal Reserve action.

But what happens if the Federal Reserve *sells* securities instead of buying them? Then, instead of paying out checks, the Federal Reserve Banks receive checks from the buyers. When the Reserve Bank receives one of these checks, it reduces the balance on its books to the credit of the bank on which the check was drawn. In other words, here is a case in which one bank's loss has no offset in another bank's gain. To put it another way, the loss of reserves by that one bank, having no offset elsewhere in the system, is a loss of reserves for the system as a whole. This will limit the lending and investing capacity of that bank without increasing the capacity of any other bank to grant credit.

Does the Federal Reserve gain cash when it sells securities? No, it does not. The check that it receives from the buyer of the securities pulls no cash into the Federal Reserve Bank—it would do so only in the unlikely event that the Federal Reserve were paid in Treasury currency. Rather, the Federal Reserve reduces the balance on its books to the credit of the bank on which the check had been drawn. The Federal Reserve holds fewer bonds, since it sold some, but the claims of its depositors, the commercial banks, have also been reduced.

Just as purchases of securities by the Federal Reserve

raises bond prices and lowers interest rates, so the sale
of securities by the Federal Reserve will reduce bond
prices and raise interest rates. When the Reserve Banks
begin to sell, the quantity of bonds offered for sale will
be greater than it was before. In order to find buyers for
these additional bonds, the Reserve Banks will have to
offer their bonds at a price below the previous level at
which bonds were trading. This means that the sale of
securities by the Federal Reserve makes the financing of
business expansion more difficult, for it drains reserves
from the commercial banks and limits their lending
and investing capacity. It is also more expensive, for
new borrowers and others seeking cash will have to sell
their bonds at lower prices than they had previously
been able to sell them.

Indeed, the Federal Reserve authorities can adjust
their policies, not only to the general level of bond
prices, but also to the level of particular segments of the
bond markets. By buying or selling bonds of different
maturities, they can influence the spread in interest
yields on short-term bonds as compared with long-term
bonds.

The Federal Reserve Banks buy and sell U.S. Government securities to the exclusion of virtually all other
types of money market paper, although nominal transactions are occasionally made in short-term commercial credits known as "bankers' acceptances" and in
foreign exchange. Moreover, except under exceptional
circumstances—and then only for limited periods of
time—the Reserve Banks are prohibited from buying
Government securities directly from the Treasury: they
must buy and sell in the open market, trading there
with all other investors who deal in Government securities. The purpose of this restriction is to deny the

Treasury the temptingly easy method of financing it-self by borrowing from a quasi-governmental institu-tion—a path that has led to excessive monetary ex-pansion in many other countries. Instead, the Treasury must compete with all other borrowers in the market-place for the investment funds of individuals, corpora-tions, and financial institutions.*

Open-market purchases and sales of Treasury securi-ties by the Federal Reserve Banks have run between 10 and 20 billion dollars annually in recent years—about 5 to 10 per cent of total activity in the Government se-curity market.

The basic policy decisions as to the magnitude, tim-ing, and selection of Federal Reserve operations are set by the Federal Open Market Committee in Wash-ington, consisting of the seven members of the Board of Governors, the President of the Federal Reserve Bank of New York (where the actual transactions for System accounts are made), and the Presidents of four other Federal Reserve Banks (who serve one year each and then yield to the Presidents of four other Reserve Banks). The Committee usually meets once every three weeks to review the state of the economy in gen-eral and monetary conditions in particular, and to set fresh operating instructions for the officers charged with the day-to-day application of Committee policy.

The day-to-day execution of Committee policy is no simple matter. In the first place, a large part of open-market operations is concerned with adjusting aberra-tions that develop in the supply of member bank re-serves, owing to factors that have nothing whatever to

* This restriction also completely separates decisions relating to the regulation of bank credit and the money supply from the wholly different set of decisions concerned with Treasury financing and debt management.

do with monetary policy as such—inflows and outflows of currency, Treasury receipts and disbursements, the movement across the country of checks in the process of clearing, and so on.* Offsetting the impact of these factors requires a fine touch and accurate forecasts in their trends, so that changes in member bank reserves in line with fundamental policy can take place smoothly rather than abruptly or in a disjointed manner.

Second, since it consists of human beings who recognize their fallibility as economic prognosticators, the Committee is always reluctant to pursue any policy too far or too fast. Thus, policy is executed in a tentative manner, a little at a time, with breathing spells to see how much effect it is having and whether basic economic conditions are moving in the anticipated direction. The result is that Committee operating instructions tend to be masterpieces of "on-the-one-hand-on-the-other-hand" language. The following is an example:

> It is the current policy of the Federal Open Market Committee to permit the supply of bank credit and money to increase further, but at the same time to avoid redundant bank reserves that would [depress interest rates and] encourage capital outflows internationally.
> Operations of the System Open Market Account during the next three weeks shall be conducted with a view to providing moderate reserve expansion in the banking system but also to fostering a moderately firm tone [i.e. steady to rising interest rates] in money markets.

But the Federal Reserve can do more than step into the breach by buying securities when all banks are short on reserves. Just as the Federal Reserve will buy when no one else has sufficient cash available, so the Reserve

* These factors are fully discussed in subsequent chapters and in the Appendix.

Banks can make loans to member banks when no other bank has sufficient excess reserves to do so.

The essential principle involved is the same. When one bank borrows from another, reserves are transferred from the lending bank to the borrowing bank; one has more, the other less; the two together have the same amount of reserves that they had to begin with. If one bank borrows from the Federal Reserve, however, the Federal Reserve will increase the balance on its books to the credit of that bank: the borrowing bank will have more, but no other bank will have less. No cash will leave the Federal Reserve as a result of this loan, for if the borrowing bank subsequently loses those reserves, either because it buys securities with them or because its depositors draw out more than they put in, the reserves lost by that bank will simply be transferred to some other bank. The sums on the books of the Federal Reserve to the credit of the various banks will shift from bank to bank, but no cash will be withdrawn from the Federal Reserve Banks.

Only banks that are members of the Federal Reserve System can borrow from Federal Reserve Banks. Furthermore, the Federal Reserve authorities consider this a privilege, not a right. In other words, although the member banks will of course take the initiative in deciding whether or not they want to borrow from the Federal Reserve, the Federal Reserve can always refuse to approve the loan.

For example, they will refuse to give credit if a bank appears to be injudiciously overextended and should therefore liquidate securities or make fewer loans. They will refuse if a bank borrows for too long a period of time, and, in effect, uses the money borrowed from the Federal Reserve, instead of its depositors' or stockholders' money, to finance its lending and investing operations. In the words of the Board of Governors, Reserve Bank credit is generally extended to a member bank, "because of developments such as a sudden withdrawal of deposits or seasonal requirements for credit beyond those which can reasonably be met by use of the bank's own resources . . . [or] in meeting unusual situations . . . or exceptional circumstances."

Borrowing from a Federal Reserve Bank is usually known as "discounting" and is customarily secured by U.S. Government securities put up as collateral. The Federal Reserve Banks naturally charge interest for these loans, the interest rate being known as the "discount rate."

As a general rule, the Federal Reserve Banks almost never keep the discount rate far below the rate of return on short-term Treasury securities. This would encourage an excessive amount of borrowing, as banks would use the reserves borrowed at a low rate to invest in (or refrain from selling) securities earning a higher rate of return. As a matter of fact, the discount rate is usually just about equal to or higher than the yield on U.S. Treasury bills—highly liquid obligations of the U.S. Government, maturing every ninety days. The higher the discount rate relative to the bill rate, of course, the more reluctant the banks will be to borrow and the greater the frequency with which they will sell securities to replenish their reserve positions.

This indicates how effective discount-rate policy can be. When the discount rate is low relative to the bill rate, banks that are short on reserves will be encouraged to borrow from the Federal Reserve Banks in preference to selling securities. Thus, they will put no pressure on the reserve positions of other banks, for, if they sold securities, they would be receiving checks drawn by the buyers on other banks, reserves would shift from these banks to the bank selling the securities, and the shortage of reserves would spread. Borrowing from the Federal Reserve prevents a shortage of reserves in some banks from spreading to others.

However, when the discount rate is high relative to the yield on securities, banks will be reluctant to borrow and will prefer to replenish a short reserve position by selling securities. Unless the Open Market Committee comes to the rescue and buys those securities, a shortage of reserves in some banks will tend to spread throughout the system.

Therefore, although the Federal Reserve authorities can never force banks to come to the discount window, nor can they justifiably deny a *bona fide* request by a member bank for accommodation on a temporary basis, the discount rate can nevertheless be an effective means of relieving or of intensifying a shortage of member bank reserves. Indeed, the trend in member bank borrowings is a sensitive indicator of whether banks feel they have sufficient or insufficient reserves; the persistence of a trend in one direction or another is a useful guide to the policy the Reserve authorities may be attempting to pursue.

Thus, open-market operations and discount policy can exert a strong influence on the volume of member bank reserves and, thereby, on member bank lending and investing—and, ultimately, on the quantity of money in the economy.

However, while an increase in member bank borrowings from the Federal Reserve shows that the banks are trying to maintain their lending and investing operations, and while a fall in member bank borrowings shows that the banks have accumulated more reserves than they need at that particular mo-

ment, Federal Reserve open-market operations reflect
the initiative of the Federal Reserve authorities in attempting to influence the member banks to restrict or
expand their loans and security holdings. The important difference is that the ebb and flow of member
bank borrowings show the efforts of the banks to
maintain the *status quo*, whereas Federal Reserve open-
market operations are an effort to change it.

Since the purchases and sales of Government securities by the Federal Reserve Banks represent the
active, rather than the passive, arm of monetary policy,
their impact on the economy is more interesting for us
to analyze.

When the Reserve Banks go into the market and buy
securities, they have to find someone who is willing to
sell. In order to induce investors to sell securities, the
Reserve Banks must offer to pay higher prices than those
currently prevailing or must be willing to buy more
than had previously been bid for at current prices. In
either case, the initial effect of the Federal Reserve purchases is to persuade some investor to hold money instead of securities. At the same time, reserves will be
gained by the banks in which the sellers of the securities maintain their checking accounts. Banks gaining
reserves will tend to respond initially by going out and
buying securities (or by refraining from selling some
that they might otherwise have liquidated), so that
further amounts of money will be substituted for the
security holdings of individuals and corporations.

What do the former holders of securities do with the
money they have now received? Some of them perhaps
sold their securities because they expected bond prices
to decline in the future; others sold because they
needed the money to finance their businesses or to pay
for goods and services they wanted to buy. The first

group, finding the banks eagerly bidding for securities, will see that their expectations of bond prices were mistaken and will probably use the money to make some fresh investment. As Government securities and other high-quality bonds rise in price, investors will begin to look at lower-quality bonds and at common stocks that appear relatively attractive now that the safest types of investments are more expensive than they were before.

To use a technical term, the liquidity of the economy has increased: people are holding more money than they had been holding, and those who need cash find it easier to raise through selling securities or finding a willing lender. Although this situation in itself gives no assurance that individuals or business firms will use this additional liquidity to go out and buy more goods and services than they had been buying (which presumably was the objective that motivated the Federal Reserve open-market purchases in the first place), money ultimately does begin to burn a hole in most people's pockets. Furthermore, any increased demand for goods and services that does develop can now be much more readily financed.

When, on the other hand, the Reserve Banks are sellers of securities, they must find investors willing to buy; this means they must offer securities at prices lower than those currently prevailing. Furthermore, the banks in which the buyers of the securities maintain their accounts will lose reserves and will also have to sell securities (or refrain from buying them). By offering securities at lower prices, then, the Reserve Banks and the commercial banks are in effect persuading investors to part with money and to take securities instead. And this trend spreads throughout the financial community. With Government bonds at lower prices, lesser quality

bonds and common stocks look more expensive than
they had previously appeared, and their prices tend to
drop as well. Individuals and businessmen needing
cash find it more difficult to raise and are more reluctant to increase their spending for goods and services.
They may even be forced to retrench their activities.

Through this complicated, frequently tortuous, and
largely indirect process, monetary policy attempts to
influence the level of business activity. As we saw at the
very beginning of this book, we must be sure that we
have enough money to buy everything that we can produce but never so much that we try to buy substantially
more than we can produce. All that monetary policy
can do is to put money into people's pockets or to persuade them to give up money in exchange for securities; thereby the authorities hope to induce the rate of
spending for goods and services to rise or to fall. But
people may be reluctant to spend this additional
money or, in the opposite case, may still be able to
finance their expenditures without too much trouble.
We shall in subsequent chapters see the extent to
which this process actually works.

Meanwhile, however, the Federal Reserve authorities have another string to their bow, with broader implications that justify our devoting an entire chapter
to it.

CHAPTER IX

Reserve Requirements

When the Federal Reserve System was established in 1913, the discount rate was the only genuine tool of monetary policy with which the authorities were supposed to work. The impact of open-market operations, on the other hand, was discovered more or less by accident: the Reserve Banks started buying Government securities with their excess funds, as any bank would, and then noticed that they were increasing the supply of member bank reserves. Today's sophisticated and highly organized use of open-market operations was developed to some extent during the late 1920's and the 1930's, but came into its own only after World War II.

After the disasters of 1929–33, new legislation was passed in Congress to improve the operation of the Fed-

eral Reserve System and to widen still further the pow-
ers of the Reserve Banks and the Board of Governors.
One of the major additions effected in the Banking Act
of 1935 was the permanent grant to the Board of the
power to vary member bank reserve requirements—to
raise or to lower the amount that each bank had to keep
in legal reserves in relation to the volume of deposits it
has outstanding. The higher this requirement, the
smaller the amount of any given level of cash resources
that the banks can lend and invest; the lower the reserve requirement, the greater the amount of credit and
new money that the member banks can create from a
given volume of reserves.

At the end of 1963, member banks in large cities and
financial centers—so-called "reserve city banks"—were
required either to have currency in their vaults or to
carry deposits at their local Federal Reserve Banks in an
amount equal to at least 16½ per cent of their demand
deposits and 4 per cent of their time and savings deposits. Banks in smaller cities and rural areas—so-called
"country banks"—had the same requirement with re-
spect to time and savings deposits (which account for a
much larger proportion of total deposits in rural than
in urban areas), but the reserve requirement against
checking accounts was smaller than for reserve city
banks—12 per cent, to be exact.

Changes in reserve requirements have occurred much
less frequently than changes in the discount rate or in
open-market policy. An increase or decrease in reserve
requirements is a blunt instrument: it hits all banks at
once across the board, whether they have ample supplies
of reserves or whether they are all loaned up. The use
of discount rate changes or open-market operations, on
the other hand, tends to facilitate adjustments at those
banks that are short of reserves or have too much cash,

without having those adjustments drain reserves away from other banks or flood other banks with an excessive amount of reserves.

Therefore, while major changes or changes that are to take effect in a short period of time can be accomplished with a variation in reserve requirements, the System authorities have found that they can do a much better job most of the time in fine-tuning the supply of member bank reserves through open-market operations and discount policy.

Nevertheless, the reserve requirement, whether constant or changing, is extremely important. It sets an upper limit to the amounts that each bank can lend and invest, which means in turn that it sets an upper limit to the supply of money itself. Although reserve requirements were originally established to make certain that each bank would have adequate cash on hand to meet withdrawals by its depositors, their real significance today lies in their use as a tool to control the supply of money.

Up to this point, we have analyzed the operations of the banking system on the assumption that each banker more or less sets his own reserve requirement. In other words, we have seen that each individual bank will be reluctant to lend or invest all of the cash it has on hand or at the Federal Reserve, because money lent out will soon be withdrawn by the borrower and securities purchased must be paid for at once. Lending and investing therefore lead to an outflow of reserves from the bank, and, if carried too far, will leave the bank with no reserves to cover withdrawals that its depositors may make in excess of the amounts they are depositing.

The introduction of the reserve requirement changes the form of this picture of the individual bank, but it does little to change the substance. Now each bank must hold not only enough available reserves to cover net withdrawals by depositors, but also enough to satisfy the requirement set by the Federal Reserve. Rather than looking at the total reserves to see how much a bank might lend and invest, we must rather look only to the *excess* reserve that the bank has available over and above the amount stipulated by the Reserve authorities.

Take, for example, the case of a bank with total demand deposits of $1,000,000. If it is a reserve city bank, it will be required to have currency in its vaults plus a deposit at the Federal Reserve Bank totalling at least $165,000, or 16½ per cent of its demand deposits. If it has exactly that amount, it has no money available to lend or invest. If it has more than that, it can at least consider increasing its loans or security holdings. If it has less, it will either have to liquidate some of its securities in order to increase its reserve balance, or it will have to borrow reserves—most probably from the Federal Reserve Bank.*

Unless a bank is expecting its deposits to increase, its management will probably want to carry a reserve balance in excess of the stipulated minimum. If the bank has deposits of $1,000,000 and reserves of precisely $165,000, it will be in trouble if net withdrawals occur. If its depositors now withdraw $100,000 more than they deposit, this bank's vault cash and balance at the Fed-

---

* As a practical matter, banks do not have to meet the reserve requirement every single day, but they do have to cover it on a daily *average* basis. Reserve city banks must have a daily average of reserves sufficient to meet the requirement for each week, ending Wednesday; country banks can average out over a semimonthly period. Banks that are deficient in reserves are subject to fines and penalties, including exclusion from the privilege of borrowing at the Federal Reserve.

eral Reserve will drop to only $65,000. As its deposits have fallen to $900,000, the bank must still have 16½ per cent of $900,000 in reserve, and that works out to $148,500—far more than the $65,000 actually on hand. Even if the depositors withdraw only $10, rather than $100,000, the principle is the same: the amount of reserves the bank is required to hold will go down only $1.65 but its actual reserves will drop by $10. That is why some excess reserve balance is absolutely essential if depositors are likely to be pulling money out of the bank.

The introduction of the reserve requirement changes fundamentally the limits within which the banking system as a whole can operate. From the viewpoint of monetary policy, this is its real significance. Let us see how it works out.

We have already seen that, while each individual bank will lose reserves when it lends and invests, the system as a whole does *not* lose reserves—the reserves lost by one bank are deposited in another. Therefore, while each bank is limited by its available cash resources in how much it can lend and invest, no limit exists (in theory, at least*) to the amount that the banking system as a whole can lend and invest. This means that the money supply could increase to an infinite amount.

This would be close to true in actual practice if the country were served by one big bank with about 14,000

---

* Practical limitations do indeed exist. They are discussed in detail in Chapter X. Among other things, the public may use the additional demand deposits they receive to acquire time deposits in commercial banks or to repurchase securities from the commercial banks. For a further discussion of this important point, see Tobin, J., "Commercial Banks as Creators of 'Money'," *Banking and Monetary Studies*, edited by Deane Carson (Homewood, Ill.: Richard D. Irwin, 1963).

branches, instead of by 14,000 individual banks, each making its own individual decisions. Since this big bank would never lose reserves—its master bookkeeping computer would only note a shift in reserves from one branch to another—it could lend out and invest as much as it wished. The withdrawals made by borrowers would be deposited in other offices of the bank, as the checks they issued were deposited by the people who received them. Similarly, the checks issued by the bank for the securities it bought would also be deposited in one or another of its offices. Since it would never have to worry about losing cash to some other bank, it would have no theoretical limit to how far it could go. It could simply disregard the problem of reserves.

But if we impose a minimum reserve requirement on this giant bank, we also limit the extent to which it can continue to make loans and buy securities. For example, the bank might have 100 billion dollars in deposits and 25 billion dollars in reserves. If we set the reserve requirement at 20 per cent (to make the arithmetic a little simpler than if we used the 16½ per cent figure), the bank would have 5 billion dollars in reserves over and above the required 20 billion dollars. Clearly a point must come when deposits will have risen to a point where 25 billion dollars in reserves will just meet the requirement, with no excess reserve left over.

Would we be correct in saying that the bank could increase its loans and investments by 5 billion dollars, an amount precisely equal to its excess reserves? No, the bank can go further than that. If it lends and invests 5 billion dollars, its deposits will increase from 100 billion dollars to 105 billion dollars. Against 105 billion dollars it must hold 21 billion dollars—still leaving 4 billion dollars excess. If the bank therefore lends out another 4 billion, it will increase the borrowers' accounts by 4 billion dollars and deposits will reach 109 billion dollars. As 20 per cent of this is 21.8 billion, excess reserves are still available to the tune of 3.2 billion dollars.

Now the management of the bank sees how far it can go. It goes out and buys up precisely 16 billion dollars more in securities. Why precisely that amount? The people who sell those securities receive checks from the bank, which of course they deposit in their accounts and which will bring total deposits up to 125 billion dollars. The amount of reserves the bank must hold against 125 billion dollars works out to 25 billion dollars, exactly the amount on hand. We have reached the limit of the process. With the reserve requirement at 20 per cent, or one fifth of the amount on deposit in checking accounts, the bank's deposits can rise to a maximum of five times the amount in reserves—five times 25 billion dollars in this case. At any point when the bank has excess reserves, the potential expansion left will be equal to five times the excess reserves (when the reserve requirement is 20 per cent), as the deposits in our example increased from 100 billion dollars to 125 billion dollars on excess reserves of 5 billion dollars. If the reserve requirement were 16½ per cent, the expansion could be sixfold, four times if the requirement were 25 per cent, and so on.

Now, no individual bank can come anywhere near lending out five times its excess reserves. If a bank has $1,000,000 in deposits and $250,000 in reserves, of which $200,000 must be held to meet the reserve requirement, it can lend out $50,000 as a theoretical maximum. As the borrowers will soon withdraw the proceeds of the loan, this bank can afford to lose no more than $50,000 in reserves if it is to avoid falling below the minimum required. If it lent or invested $250,000, five times its excess reserves, it would soon lose its entire reserve balance and would be far below the Reserve's requirement—to say nothing of being unable to meet any further withdrawals by its depositors.

Nevertheless, although each individual bank is limited by its excess reserves to what it can lend and invest, the system as a whole, just like the big nationwide bank, can lend and invest many times the excess reserves held by all the banks.

This can work out as follows, if we begin with our bank that has $1,000,000 in deposits and $50,000 in excess reserves: If the bank lends $50,000 to one of its depositors, deposits will rise $50,000. As the borrower spends that money, the $50,000 will be deposited in other banks. Let us assume for the sake of simplicity that it goes to just one bank, which has now received a fresh deposit of $50,000 together with $50,000 in reserves transferred from the bank that made the loan. This second bank must hold at least $10,000 in reserves against its new deposit, but has $40,000 in excess reserves that it can lend and invest.

If this second bank now buys $40,000 in securities, it will issue a check to the buyer. The buyer will deposit that check in his account at a third bank, as a result of which total deposits in the system will have risen by $40,000. This third bank has also gained $40,000 in reserves and can lend out or invest $32,000, keeping back $8000 to satisfy the reserve requirement against its new deposit.

Up to this point, the original $50,000 in excess reserves is now distributed among three banks—one holding $10,000 against a new deposit of $50,000, one holding $8000 against a new deposit of $40,000, and a third that has just received the $32,000 that the second bank either lent or invested. This means that the original

$50,000 has made possible a total of $50,000 + $40,000 + $32,000, or $122,000 in loans and investments, with more yet to come.

And so the process continues, as each bank receives new deposits from other banks as a result of the expenditures of borrowers or the purchases of securities by banks with excess reserves. Since each bank receiving the new deposits has to hold part of the accompanying reserves to satisfy the reserve requirement, the amount that each successive bank can lend or invest grows smaller and smaller, but the process will continue until every bank in the system has used up its excess reserves and is "loaned up." In the end, the result is no different from the computation we did for the giant bank— the potential increase in bank credit will be a predictable multiple of the starting amount of excess reserves.

We can now see how the whole range of Federal Reserve instruments of control can operate.

The lower the amount each bank has to hold in reserves, the greater the amount it can lend out and invest. In other words, the lower the reserve requirement, the larger the expansion of loans and investments in the banking system can be and, therefore, the greater the probable increase in the quantity of money in the economy. With the reserve requirement at the end of 1963 at 16½ per cent, every dollar of additional excess reserves could theoretically lead to an expansion of $6 in demand deposits.

Although the reserve requirement will determine what proportion of a given level of bank reserves is available for loans and investments, it tells us nothing about whether the banks actually have reserves above or below the amounts they are required to hold. This total quantity of reserves will be influenced and deter mined by discount policy and open-market operations.

Thus, when the Federal Reserve believes that member banks have too little in reserve over and above what is required ("too little" meaning that the authorities would like to see the supply of money increase), they will lower the discount rate and buy Government securities in the open market. When they believe that bank credit is advancing too rapidly and that the expanding money supply is financing an inflationary spiral, they may raise reserve requirements, thereby stipulating that a smaller amount of a given level of reserves is available for loans and investments, or they may raise the discount rate and sell Government securities.*

In actual practice, the Reserve authorities watch the level of member bank excess reserves in relation to member bank borrowings from the Federal Reserve Banks. When excess reserves are greater than borrowings, this difference is known as "free reserves"; when borrowings run above excess reserves, the difference is known as "negative free reserves." The reason for watching free reserves as a measure of likely bank decisions to lend or invest is that reserves gained by banks through borrowing from the Federal Reserve Banks are temporary in character; they will probably be paid off and disappear in the near future. A bank with a large debt to the Federal Reserve will be reluctant to expand its loans and

---

* On some occasions, the Federal Reserve has bought Government securities at the same time that it raised reserve requirements. An increase in reserve requirements may leave some banks with less in reserve than they need to meet the stipulated minimum. They will therefore tend to liquidate securities to restore their cash position. Other investors, anticipating this development, may also sell securities in the belief that security prices will decline as a consequence of Federal Reserve policy. In order to cushion this decline and prevent a speculative panic, therefore, the Federal Reserve may temporarily bolster the Government security market by entering as a buyer.

investments until it has gained sufficient reserves to bring itself out of debt.

The excess reserves in the commercial banking system are held primarily by banks in small cities and rural centers. Reserve city banks normally keep their available cash employed right up to the limit; consequently, they are frequent borrowers at the Federal Reserve. Therefore, the trend of free reserves, though important, is actually the result of varying practices among banks in vastly different economic and financial environments.

Nevertheless, the swing in these items can be substantial. Although we shall take up a more detailed survey of the actual course of events in Part Four, the following table shows what has happened at selected dates to some of the magnitudes (in billions of dollars) that we have been discussing:

	Total reserves	Excess reserves	Borrowed reserves	Free reserves
All member banks				
December 1954	19.3	0.7	0.2	0.5
December 1959	18.9	0.5	0.9	−0.4
December 1963	20.7	0.5	0.3	0.2
Country banks				
December 1954	5.6	0.6	0.1	0.5
December 1959	6.0	0.5	0.2	0.3
December 1963	7.3	0.4	0.1	0.3
Reserve city banks				
December 1954	13.7	0.1	0.1	*
December 1959	12.9	*	0.7	−0.7
December 1963	13.4	0.1	0.2	−0.1

* Less than 500 million dollars.

Note that the total supply of reserves changed relatively little and that the volume of excess reserves was also more or less constant. But, between the end of 1954 and the end of 1959, in response to the sharp economic expansion of the second half of the 1950's, loans at New York, Chicago, and other reserve city banks expanded from 39 billion dollars to 61 billion dollars. Selling off Government securities financed 10 billion dollars of this, but in any case deposits in these banks expanded by 14 billion dollars. As a result, of course, the amounts of cash the banks had to hold in reserve also increased sharply. Since the total volume of reserves available to them held steady and they had little or no excess reserve to begin with, they had to find the additional reserves to meet the reserve requirement by borrowing the necessary sums from the Federal Reserve Banks.

As the borrowings from the Federal Reserve grew larger, the banks became increasingly reluctant to extend themselves further. Thus, the Federal Reserve authorities, eager to snuff out what they believed was an intensifying inflationary potential in the economy, managed to put the brakes on the expansion in the money supply. While the supply of money in the economy had risen at an annual rate of 2.2 billion dollars from 1954 through 1958, the growth during 1959 was held to only 0.8 billion.

CHAPTER X

Currency:
A Complication

Throughout this analysis, we have made an important simplifying assumption, which we should now be prepared to drop. We have stated repeatedly that withdrawals from one bank are always redeposited in some other bank in the system, so that one bank may lose reserves but the system never does. The exceptions that we have made to that rule were in those cases where the Federal Reserve sells Government securities in the open market, where member banks repay their loans to the Reserve Banks, or where the Government is taking in more money than it is paying out. In those cases one bank's loss of reserves will not be a gain for some other bank.

These exceptions, however, are the result of conscious

policy on the part of the Federal Reserve authorities, the Treasury, or the commercial banks themselves. As far as the public is concerned, we have so far permitted them to withdraw funds from one bank only on the condition that they are sure to deposit those funds in some other bank in the system.

But there is no law to make the public so obliging. Occasionally people do make withdrawals from one bank that are not offset by deposits in some other bank: this is what happens when the withdrawal takes the form of currency that circulates from hand to hand for an extended period of time. We have already noted that at Christmas time currency flows out of the banks and into the pockets of individuals and the cash registers of shopkeepers, only to return to the banks after a matter of some weeks. But this process can go on for a much longer time—during World War II, the American people drew out about 18 billion dollars in currency that was never redeposited in the banks.

Here, then, is a clear case in which the banking system as a whole can and, in fact, does lose reserves. If John Jones cashes a check for $100 to take care of the family's pocket money for a couple of weeks, and if the shops in which he spends that money pay it out as salaries to their employees, and if the employees in turn use this money for their out-of-pocket purchases, then clearly the loss of reserves by Mr. Jones's bank has no offset in a gain in reserves by some other bank. This is entirely different from the case in which Mr. Jones buys things with checks drawn on his account and the shopkeepers then deposit his checks in their accounts; in this case, the reserves lost by Mr. Jones's bank are simply transferred to his shopkeepers' banks.

This brings us back to something we noted early in this discussion, namely, that the amount of currency in circulation is not set by the Government or by any other issuing agency; rather, it is determined by the choices and habits of the public in deciding how much of their money holdings to keep in the form of currency and how much in the form of checking accounts. No law can regulate these patterns. In fact, in a crisis, when the people completely lose confidence in the banks and want to convert all of their bank deposits into currency, the system simply breaks down. In 1933, all the banks were forced by the Government to close their doors until confidence was gradually restored.

If the needs and habits of the public are to be satisfied, and if the system is to work smoothly without such breakdowns, two conditions are necessary: First, the banks themselves have to be able to sustain the loss in reserves that results from an outflow of currency. They must either have sufficient excess reserve balances to be able to lose reserves without having to call in their loans or liquidate their securities, or some mechanism must exist to replenish their reserve balances as an offset to the loss caused by the currency withdrawals. Otherwise, outflows of currency will force the banks to curtail or reduce their lending and investing, which in turn will shrink the total supply of money and greatly intensify the difficulties of financing business expansion.

The second necessary condition is that the physical supply of currency itself should be large enough to satisfy the needs of the public. Had the 18 billion dollars in additional currency been unavailable during the war, the experiences of our earlier history would have been repeated, in which currency actually circulated at a premium—$1 in currency would buy more than $1 paid by check.

Indeed, our past history was checkered with mone-

tary crises brought about by an insufficiently elastic supply of currency or by bank failures and money panics
resulting from the loss of reserves that accompanied sustained currency withdrawals. But, once again, the Federal Reserve has come to the rescue—in fact, preventing
a recurrence of such circumstances was one of the major
reasons for the establishment of the Federal Reserve
System in the first place.

We have already seen that the Reserve authorities
have the ability to increase the supply of member bank
reserves when they consider it necessary to do so. By
making the discount window available to banks losing
reserves due to currency withdrawals and by purchasing
Government securities in the open market, the Reserve
Banks can replenish bank reserves to a point where no
undesirable liquidation of bank loans and investments
will be necessary.

Thus, for example, total member bank reserves actually *increased* by more than 3 billion dollars during
World War II, despite the outflow of 18 billion dollars in currency, for the Federal Reserve Banks purchased on balance over 20 billion dollars in Government securities and increased their loans to member
banks at the same time.

We can see the opposite process at work in the after-
math of the Christmas shopping season of 1962. During
January 1963, 1.4 billion dollars in currency flowed back
into the banks and out of circulation. This should have
increased member bank reserves by a like amount, but
member bank reserves at the end of January were, in
fact, 700 million dollars less than they had been at the
end of December. The reason was that the Reserve
Banks were net sellers of Government securities during
January, while the member banks reduced their bor-

rowings from the Federal Reserve Banks from over 700 million to only 100 million dollars.

But this brings us to our second problem, which is where all this currency comes from to begin with. We know that we obtain currency by cashing checks and thereby reducing our deposits at commercial banks, but where do they get the currency they pay out to us? And we also know that we replenish our checking accounts by redepositing currency when we have more on hand than we need, but what do the banks do with that currency they receive from us? Borrowers and people from whom the banks buy securities would be most reluctant to take currency in payment for sums of that character —and would be most unlikely to use currency to repay loans or to pay for securities the banks sell.

The answer to these questions lies once again with the Federal Reserve Banks, whose relationship with the commercial banks, as we have stressed, is precisely the same as the relationship between the commercial banks and the public. When the banks must provide currency to the public, they will draw down their deposits at the Federal Reserve Banks and the Reserve Banks will then deliver the currency to the member banks. When currency flows back into the banking system from the public, the member banks will send the currency back to the Federal Reserve Banks and replenish their deposits there.

But have we really advanced this argument at all? First of all, where do the Federal Reserve Banks obtain the currency they provide for the member banks? Second, if the member banks lose reserves when they have to pay out currency to the public, and may thereby be forced to curtail their lending and investing activities, won't the same thing be true of the Federal Reserve

Banks? Won't the outflow of currency from the Federal Reserve Banks hamper their ability to come to the rescue of the member banks through discounting and open-market purchases of securities? Who comes to the rescue of the Federal Reserve?

The original Federal Reserve Act in 1913 established a form of paper currency called the Federal Reserve Note, which accounts for most of the money the Reserve Banks provide when called upon for currency. Out of a total of 37 billion dollars of currency and coin in circulation at the end of 1963, 32 billion dollars—seven out of every eight dollars—were accounted for by Federal Reserve Notes. The balance was coin and paper currency issued by the Treasury, of which nearly 2 billion dollars in currency redeemable in silver was gradually being replaced by Federal Reserve Notes.

The trick in the Federal Reserve Notes is that the Federal Reserve Banks lose no cash when they pay out this currency to the member banks. Federal Reserve Notes are not redeemable in anything except what the Government calls "legal tender"—that is, money that a creditor must be willing to accept from a debtor in payment of sums owed him. But since all Federal Reserve Notes are themselves declared by law to be legal money, they are really redeemable only in themselves! To put it briefly, they are an irredeemable obligation issued by the Federal Reserve Banks.

Does it seem surprising that nearly 90 per cent of the currency we use is really worth no more than the paper on which it is printed? It should be no more surprising than the fact that the coins we use contain metal worth substantially less than the face value of the coins. Nor, indeed, should it be more surprising than our willingness to use checking accounts as money to a much greater extent than we use currency—for what is the "backing" for checking accounts?

The backing for checking accounts is to be found in the assets of the commercial banks in which we maintain these deposits. And what do they consist of? At least three quarters of these assets are loans to individuals and business firms and marketable obligations issued by corporations and governmental agencies. Their soundness rests upon the soundness of each individual borrower—but the ultimate soundness of the borrowers depends upon the level of prosperity and rate of economic growth throughout the American economy. The balance of the assets of the commercial banks is listed as cash—which means this same irredeemable currency plus deposits with the Federal Reserve Banks. But the deposits with the Reserve Banks are redeemable only in currency again, so that the cash assets end up looking little more substantial than the loans and investments.

In short, the money that we use every day, the money that we are all happy to accept in payment for goods sold, services rendered, and debts incurred, is intrinsically worthless: it has no tangible backing, in the strict sense of the word. Yet, though it has no value of its own, we nevertheless value it highly! We value it because of what we have to give up to get it—our labor and our possessions—and because of what we can buy with it. The real meaning of the value of our money, in other words, is how much a dollar can buy. The dollar is worth a lot because we can buy a lot with it, but money is worthless in economies flooded with money and short on goods—which is why we evoke the uneasy early days of our history and say something is "not worth a Continental."

Tangible money is just as "worthless" as intangible

money, when we really get right down to it. Men worship and treasure gold, but the Midas story reminds us that he who has only gold is truly poverty-stricken. If the young United States had been flooded with gold instead of with paper money after the Revolution in 1783, we would have been just as badly off as we were with the Continental currency, because there was so little available to buy and so much money around to spend.

The only real attraction of gold as a basis for a monetary system is that its supply is limited, or at least increases slowly, whereas only the judgments and fallibility of men can put a limit to the issuance of money based on credit and promises. The use of something like gold, in other words, will tend to prevent us from having too much money in relation to the supply of things we want to buy (although substantial inflations did in fact occur despite the existence of the old gold standard). However, it also may set too low the upper limit on the money supply, in which case we will have too little money and will be unable to finance business expansion and economic growth. This situation has often proved intolerable. After all, gold has no power of its own, only the power with which men endow it, so that we have repeatedly thrown off the shackles imposed by gold whenever they interfered too much with the economic objectives we have pursued.*

To return to the main thread of our argument, the member banks obtain the currency they need to supply the demands of the public by withdrawing that currency from the Federal Reserve Banks, and the Federal Reserve Banks simply issue that currency in exchange for the deposits the member banks carry with them as

* A full discussion of gold follows in Part Four.

legal reserves. When currency outstanding goes up, member bank reserve balances at the Federal Reserve Banks go down. When the public redeposits currency, the member banks in turn redeposit it at the Federal Reserve Banks and replenish their reserve accounts there. But while the member banks lose reserves when they pay out currency, the Federal Reserve Banks do not.

If, as once was the case, the member banks could also issue paper currency (as, in fact, they now "issue" demand deposits in payment for loans granted and securities purchased), then they could give their own notes to the public and would lose no cash at such times. This procedure is now prohibited by law, however: only the Treasury and the Federal Reserve are allowed to issue currency and only their notes are given the blessing of legal tender that makes them acceptable everywhere in the nation.

One point about this is particularly important to keep in mind. We speak of the Federal Reserve Banks as "issuing" Federal Reserve Notes. In a manner of speaking, they do issue these notes, because the notes have their imprint and they enter circulation from the vaults of the Reserve Banks. On the other hand, the word "issue" implies that the Reserve Banks somehow put them into circulation. As we know, this is not the case at all: currency moves out into circulation in response to the demands and requirements of the public, when and as people choose to use more of their money in the form of currency and less in the form of checking accounts. No bank and no governmental agency can determine the direction or the limits of those choices.

When we look back over the ground that we have covered and ask what the American dollar is really based upon, we would have to say that it exists essentially on promises and bookkeeping machines. If anyone were to set up such a system by decree or legislation, it would probably never work. Indeed, it is just as well that most people never stop to realize that the money they earn for their efforts is only a number in a bookkeeping machine or a piece of paper convertible into nothing more than another number in a bookkeeping machine.

But are there any limits to it? Can the Federal Reserve create member bank reserves and issue currency until they reach infinity? What safeguards exist to keep us from being drowned in a flood of money? Yes, there are limits, set by gold. How satisfactorily these limits work, however, is something else again and will be pursued more fully in Part Four.

Part Four

GOLD

CHAPTER XI

Gold at Home

During all the preceding analysis of the workings of our monetary system, gold has appeared to play no role at all. Now, after waiting so long in the wings to determine the ultimate course of the drama, gold steps into the center of the stage.

For under present rules and regulations, the ultimate barrier to the expansion of member bank reserves and the supply of Federal Reserve Notes is set by gold: it thereby sets the upper limit to the amount of money that can exist in the United States.

As matters stand now, the note and deposit liabilities
of the Federal Reserve Banks must not exceed four
times their holdings of gold certificates, a special form
of currency backed 100 per cent by gold actually held
in the Treasury vaults at Fort Knox, Kentucky. For example, at the end of 1963, member bank reserve balances and other deposit accounts (mostly of the U.S.
Treasury) at the Federal Reserve Banks totalled 18.4
billion dollars and Federal Reserve notes outstanding
amounted to 32.4 billion dollars. Against this total of
50.8 billion dollars in liabilities, the Reserve Banks were
required to have at least one fourth as much—12.7
billion dollars—in gold certificates. Actual gold certificate reserves came to 15.2 billion dollars, leaving an
excess reserve of 2.5 billion dollars.

This is rather a narrow margin of safety. Back in
1941, gold certificate reserves amounted to more than
20 billion dollars and deposit and note liabilities to
only about 25 billion dollars, so that an enormous potential existed for expanding the credit base.* In the
intervening years, however, both sides of the equation
have undergone a radical change. The volume of Federal Reserve Notes outstanding has almost tripled, reflecting the vast growth in the money supply during the
war and postwar years. Helped along by tremendous
purchases of Government securities by the Federal Reserve Banks, member bank reserves have risen 50 per
cent: this rise has made possible the expansion in bank
credit and, consequently, in the money supply that we
shall study in detail in Part Five. Finally, for reasons
that we shall also be exploring shortly, the United

---

* Until 1945, the reserve requirement of the Federal Reserve
Banks was 35 per cent against deposit liabilities and 40 per cent
against notes. At the end of the war, however, these requirements
were dropped to a flat 25 per cent against the total of both.

States has been losing gold to foreign countries, especially since 1957.

A continuation of these trends—a loss of Federal Reserve Bank gold certificate reserves on the one hand, and an expansion in currency outstanding and in the member bank reserve base on the other—would soon cause the upper limits to be reached. At that time, the Federal Reserve would be unable to purchase any more Government securities on balance or to increase loans to member banks. This means that member bank reserves could no longer increase and would, in fact, have to shrink if currency in circulation continued to expand. And that, in turn, would mean that an upper limit to the money supply would have been reached as well.

Two escape hatches remain open, however, if a further increase in the money supply to finance business expansion appears desirable when these limits are reached. First, the Federal Reserve can lower member bank reserve requirements, so that, with the same volume of reserves, banks can lend out and invest larger sums than they can under present conditions. Second, the Board of Governors of the Federal Reserve System has the authority to suspend the Reserve Banks' 25 per cent gold certificate reserve requirement for a period not exceeding thirty days and then on renewal for successive periods not exceeding fifteen days each.*

As a practical matter, as opposed to the political and emotional factors involved, we are therefore still some distance from the end of the line. But the important point here is that the outflow of gold from the United States, which is related primarily to our financial re-

---

* Of course Congress can change the law any time, which is precisely what they did after this book was published. Now the reserve requirement is applied only against notes outstanding with none required against deposit liabilities.

lationships with foreign countries rather than to domestic economic trends, has most profound implications
for the management of our affairs at home.

But we are still left with one final brushstroke to com-
plete this portrait of our monetary system. How does
gold actually move into and out of the Treasury and
how do the gold certificates find their way into the Federal Reserve Banks?

The answer to this question lies in the unique character of gold, the only commodity we are willing to
"monetize." This means that we create new money
when we acquire gold—we just print it up and call it
gold certificates. *You don't have to have any money in
the bank to buy gold*—you just pay for it by printing
up those certificates, depositing them in your bank account, and then drawing checks against it to pay for the
gold. This may sound silly, but it is precisely what the
U.S. Government does when it acquires gold.

When we buy anything else, we have to have money
in the bank to pay for it. The money the Government
spends for intercontinental ballistic missiles, paper clips,
cement, wheat, or the salary of a Justice of the Supreme
Court has to be raised by taxation or by borrowing. The
Government, like everyone else, is prohibited from simply printing money to pay for the things it buys. Like
everyone else, the Government must somehow finance
its expenditures, must somehow obtain the funds to replenish its bank account when it falls too low.

Unless, that is, the Government is buying gold. If we
attached the mysterious qualities of gold to missiles or
paper clips or cement or wheat or Justices of the Supreme Court, the Government could also finance its
payments for those things by printing up paper money
called "missile certificates" or "paper clip certificates"

and so on. But, thank goodness, we have more important things to do with these objects than to bury them
at Fort Knox and hold them as a reserve against our currency. So we don't monetize them the way we monetize
gold.

The actual process of monetizing gold is simple
enough.

Since 1933, only the U.S. Government is allowed to
own gold (except for small quantities used for jewelry
and other industrial purposes). Americans are even for-
bidden to own gold outside the national borders of the
United States. Furthermore, the United States Government refuses to sell gold to any foreign national except
to a foreign government or a foreign central bank.*

Let us take the case in which the Treasury buys gold
from Homestake Mining, the largest company in the
business in this country. The gold comes in the form of
small bricks, about the same length and width but only
half the height of the usual building brick. Each brick
weighs more than 30 pounds. Thus, gold is an extraordinarily dense metal, a small amount of it packing a
lot of weight. A brick of this size brings $14,000 to
Homestake when it is delivered to our official cookie
jar at Fort Knox.

As in the case of any other purchase—of wheat or cement or missiles—the Government pays by issuing a
check on one of the Federal Reserve Banks. Homestake
will deposit the check in its own commercial bank account and Homestake's bank will, in turn, send the

* The expression "central bank" is a generic term that applies
to the institution in each country that exercises the general functions of the Federal Reserve System in the U.S. This is usually
the bank that holds the reserves of the commercial banks, that
issues all or most of the nation's currency, that holds its gold reserves, and serves as banker for the government.

check to the Federal Reserve Bank for deposit to its reserve account there. The Reserve Bank then reduces the Treasury's balance by $14,000. Note that the $14,000 outlay by the Government has increased Homestake's account without reducing any other account in the commercial banking system. Note, too, that Homestake's bank has gained reserves while no other bank has lost reserves. In effect, the Treasury's balance at the Federal Reserve Bank has been shifted to a member bank's account. Both the money supply and commercial bank reserves have been increased.

Does this mean that all Government spending leads to an increase in the money supply and to an increase in the reserve balances of member banks? If so, then all Government spending would appear to have an extremely inflationary impact on the economy.

But we have forgotten that the Government takes money in as well as pays it out. Most of what the Government spends is covered by taxes paid in by individuals and business firms; the balance is borrowed. Therefore, expenditures by the Government from its accounts at the Federal Reserve Banks are continuously offset by receipts of tax money or borrowed money that the Government uses to replenish its checking accounts.

Unless, once again, the item purchased happens to be gold. No one has to be taxed, no one has to lend the Government a penny in order to make possible the purchase of a little gold brick worth $14,000. The Government replenishes its account at the Federal Reserve Bank simply by printing up $14,000 in gold certificates and depositing them there, just as it would deposit any other money. That is how the gold is paid for and that is how the gold certificates come into the possession of the Federal Reserve Banks. And, therefore, the

Government can truly write checks indefinitely to pay for gold, which it can do for nothing else unless it can raise the necessary funds through taxation and borrowing.

But what happens when the United States loses gold? What happens when a foreign government decides to cash in some of its dollar balances and take the money out in the form of gold?

Insofar as the mechanics of the process are concerned, everything works precisely in reverse—except for the movement of the gold. The gold moves first from Fort Knox to New York, but the foreign buyer seldom goes to the expense and inconvenience of shipping it across the ocean. It is simply deposited for safekeeping in the vaults of the Federal Reserve Bank of New York, a great mass of a quasi-Florentine palace. There the gold resides, five stories underground, protected by an airtight and water-tight cylindrical door, 90 tons in weight.*

When the foreign government receives the gold, it issues a check on its bank account to the order of the U.S. Government. The Treasury in turn deposits this check at one of the Federal Reserve Banks. The Federal Reserve Bank will reduce the balance on its books to the credit of the bank on which the foreign government drew the check, simultaneously increasing the Treasury's balance on its books. Subsequently, the foreign government's checking account at its bank will also be reduced.†

* Gold held in safekeeping for others is called "earmarked gold."

† The foreign government or central bank may actually pay for the gold from an account at the Federal Reserve Bank, in which case nothing will happen in the commercial banking system. However, the balance that the foreign government built up at the Federal Reserve Bank had previously been accumulated by withdrawals from commercial banks.

So far this transaction has the same effect as any receipt of funds by the Treasury—both reserves and deposits of member banks are reduced and the Treasury's account at the Federal Reserve is increased.

Once again, however, the story with gold is different. Whereas the Treasury normally takes money in in order either to spend it or to use it to repay debts coming due, the money taken in from the foreign government for the sale of the gold will not be paid out again. Since the Treasury now holds less gold than it held before, gold certificates must be withdrawn from the Federal Reserve Banks and cancelled. As a result, the Treasury's balance on the books of the Federal Reserve will drop back to where it was before the gold sale, and the Reserve Banks' gold certificate reserve will be smaller.

Thus, the factors that influence the movement of gold into or out of the United States have in some ways a more profound impact on our economy than the movement of commodities that loom much larger in our day-to-day way of life, such as wheat, whiskey, and automobiles.

Of course, the two movements are intimately related, for the movement in gold is in large part determined by the trade in commodities that goes on between the United States and the rest of the world. Gold is, in fact, the strategic link between the American economy and the world around us. Our next step, therefore, is to see how business conditions abroad affect the movement of gold and, in turn, trends in business conditions at home.

CHAPTER XII

Gold Abroad

One nation cannot indefinitely pay out to foreigners more than it receives from them. This is as true of nations as it is of individuals or corporations. You can't spend money you haven't got: there has to be a day of reckoning somewhere along the line, and gold is what nations use by common consent when the day of reckoning comes. It is, in short, the only unquestioned and generally acceptable means of payment among nations, as dollars are the only unquestioned and generally acceptable means of payment among Americans, francs among Frenchmen, sterling among the British, and so on.

Few people realize, however, that gold's hegemony as the world's *sole* monetary standard has been surprisingly brief. Britain was the first country to adopt gold as the single monetary standard in 1821, but only after ample supplies of it were discovered in the latter half of the nineteenth century did most other countries follow suit. Yet by merely 1937, only about fifty years after gold had reached its zenith, not one country in the entire world continued to maintain a fixed tie between its currency and the price of gold, and only a few any longer permitted free and unlimited convertibility of their currency into gold.

The most important metamorphosis through which gold has passed since the financial catastrophes of the 1930's has been its disappearance from sight. Under the old gold standard, all other forms of money had been freely convertible into gold by all holders at fixed rates of exchange. But during the monetary collapse that followed 1929, people all over the world lost confidence in their governments' ability to maintain free convertibility into gold. What happened was the one thing that must never happen in a viable monetary system: everybody rushed to ask for conversion. The demand for gold was so much greater than its limited supply that the one thing everybody wanted was denied them and the very reason for the fear was realized: gold convertibility was suspended. Gold literally went back underground, to be seen only by the privileged few who tend it in the antiseptic vaults that have been dug for it under central banks and Treasuries throughout the world.

Once out of sight, gold began to lose some of the strange fascination it had previously held. Dubbed "part of the apparatus of conservatism" by the most famous economist of the Depression years, John Maynard Keynes, because its relatively fixed supply so rigorously set the upper limit to any expansion in the quantity of money, gold now plays a more subsidiary role

and is on the defensive against substitutes whose supply
can be more elastic for the settlement of international
accounts. This was predicted more than thirty years ago
by Keynes, in an eloquent passage from an essay en-
titled *Auri Sacra Fames:*

> Almost throughout the world, gold has been with-
> drawn from circulation. It no longer passes from hand to
> hand, and the touch of the metal has been taken away
> from men's greedy palms. The little household gods, who
> dwelt in purses and stockings and tin boxes have been
> swallowed up by a single golden image in each country,
> which lives underground and is not seen. Gold is out of
> sight—gone back into the soil. But when gods are no
> longer seen in a yellow panoply walking the earth, we
> begin to rationalise them; and it is not long before there
> is nothing left.

Thus, while gold does still set the maximum point to
which our domestic money supply can expand, only
foreign governments and central banks have the right
to convert their dollars into gold. In fact, the average
American has little or no awareness of gold's existence.
He knows that we have a hoard of it out at Fort Knox,
and that the hoard has been shrinking. He suspects this
means something is amiss, but he neither knows what is
amiss nor can he work up much concern about it.

But something *is* indeed amiss, and it *is* important to
us. For, in recent years, our gold stock has not only
been shrinking, but the claims that entitle foreign countries to ask for more of it have been increasing. If the
claims grow too large or if our gold stock falls too low,
our foreign friends may ask for gold from us, not because they need it to settle up their own international accounts, but simply because they want to be
sure to get what is coming to them before we shut
down the doors on it. Like all bankers, the United
States is able to satisfy withdrawals by some of its de-

positors some of the time but cannot satisfy withdrawals by all of its depositors at the same time.

How did the richest country in the world, holding three quarters of the world's stock of monetary gold at the end of World War II, ever get into such a position? The explanations for difficulties are easier to find than the cures: the United States has simply been paying out to foreigners more than foreigners have been paying to us.

This does not mean that we have been importing more than we have been exporting—on the contrary, our balance of trade has remained highly favorable to us. Our commercial exports of goods and services in 1963, for instance, were at a record high of 26 billion dollars; they exceeded our commercial imports by 3 billion dollars, compared with an average excess of 2.6 billion dollars during the period 1958-62.

Nor does it mean that we have been wasting our national wealth abroad—on the contrary, much of the money we have spent abroad has been used to acquire valuable and highly profitable investments. Our foreign assets now exceed 60 billion dollars, up from a mere 19 billion dollars in 1950. The annual income on these assets in 1963 was 4 billion dollars, more than enough to finance the entire increase in our long-term foreign investments in that year.

Nor does it mean that we have been giving too much of our money away to indigent foreign countries—on the contrary, 75 to 80 per cent of every dollar we give away comes right back to us as these countries buy the American goods and services they need to promote their economic development and military capabilities.

Part of our difficulty is the result of sums that we are

required to spend abroad for the maintenance and support of our own far-flung military establishment. This is unfortunately concentrated in countries that already have plenty of dollars and don't particularly need more. Despite efforts to economize on these outlays, we are still apparently required to spend on the order of 3 billion dollars annually for rent of bases and for all the various services and supplies that we buy locally.

Of course, it is impossible to point a finger at one element in our balance of payments and say that that particular item is the cause of the deficit. If eleven marbles are on one side of the scale and ten on the other, one cannot say which marble on the heavier side is causing the scale to tip—in fact, one could just as well say that the scale is tipping because of the absence of a marble on the lighter side. No, our international payments flow is out of balance because the *total* of our payments to foreigners is greater than the *total* of our receipts from them.

Here is what the actual figures looked like for 1963:

Payments Received from *Foreigners*	*Billions of dollars*
Sales of American merchandise and services	25.9
Sales of American military equipment	0.7
Income on American loans to and investments in foreign countries: Private	4.0
Government	0.5
Investments in the United States made by foreigners	0.5
Repayments of loans made by the U.S. Government to foreign countries	1.0*
Total Receipts from Foreigners	32.6

* Including 0.3 billion dollars in payments made ahead of schedule.

Payments Made to *Foreigners*

Purchases of foreign merchandise and services	22.9
Payments for maintenance of American military establishments on foreign soil	2.9
Private remittances to friends and relatives in foreign countries (including pensions)	0.8
Grants and loans made by the U.S. Government to foreign countries	4.5

Investments in foreign countries made by American individuals and corporations:

	Direct	1.7
	Security purchases	1.9
	Short-term	1.1*

Total Payments to Foreigners	35.8
Over-all U.S. Deficit (Excess of Payments)	3.2

* Including so-called "unrecorded transactions."

Although each year has its special character, the figures for 1963 as a whole are nevertheless typical of the general structure of our balance of payments in recent years. From 1950 to 1963 we paid out to foreigners a total of 29 billion dollars more than foreigners paid to us; 19 billion dollars of this cumulative deficit was incurred during the last six years of the period.

What happened to this money? How did we give it to foreigners and what did they do with it? How did it affect our monetary system and our banks?

The answers to these questions lie in the mechanics of foreign exchange transactions. Although practices and details vary, the essential character of a payment from someone in one country to someone in another country is simple enough. Let us take the case of an American who has to make a payment to an Englishman. In the normal course of events, the American holds no pounds sterling, while, also in the normal course of events, the Englishman wants payment in pounds sterling, because that is the money he uses to buy things with. What is involved, then, is the manner in which one party pays in one currency and the payee receives his money in another currency.

The American goes to his bank and pays it the necessary number of dollars, with instructions for the bank to pay the equivalent amount in sterling to the man in England. The American bank of course reduces the checking account of its American customer. Simultaneously, however, it increases the checking account on its books to the credit of an English bank that does business with it, notifying that bank of the instructions to pay the equivalent in sterling to the Englishman. The English bank, in turn, credits the necessary amount in sterling to the Englishman (or remits him a check that he deposits in his own bank, his own bank in turn collecting the necessary sterling amount from the bank that received the dollars in New York).

Thus, an Englishman has more money in the bank than he had before,* while, in the United States, dollars formerly held in American-owned checking accounts have shifted to the checking account of an English depositor.

Up to this point, the transaction has had no signifi-

* Note that this transaction increases the quantity of money in England—the increase in the Englishman's deposit did not come from a withdrawal from another Englishman's deposit but was rather a payment to him by a commercial bank, just as though the bank had purchased from him some security that he was selling. As long as the English bank continues to hold its deposit in New York, no change occurs in the supply of money in the United States. However, if the funds are withdrawn in gold, the purchase of the gold from the Treasury would result in the disappearance of a deposit in the United States.

cant effect on our monetary system—a payment of dollars has been made by one depositor to another, just as any wholly domestic payment is made.

Now, the crucial question is what the English bank is going to want to do with the dollars that it has sitting in its checking account in a New York bank. If Englishmen are spending money in the United States as fast as Americans are spending money in Britain, all will be well. The reverse of the transaction we have just seen will then take place: the English bank will instruct the American bank to pay to some American the necessary sums owed to him by an English customer, and the dollar balances will be back in the hands of Americans again. Or, perhaps, the English bank might sell those dollars to a French bank seeking dollars to cover a Frenchman's expenditures in the United States, giving the English bank francs it requires to cover an Englishman's payment to be made in France.

If, however, the United States is continuously paying out money to foreigners at a more rapid rate than foreigners have occasion to spend money here, these sums credited to the accounts of foreign banks on the books of American banks will go up and up and up. This is precisely what has been happening: deposits of foreigners in American banks plus foreign holdings of short-term securities (which can be readily liquidated and turned into bank deposits) rose about 12 billion dollars from the end of 1957 to the end of 1963, by which time they had reached a level of more than 26 billion dollars.

But why do foreigners continue to hold and accumulate those dollars? Why don't they use the dollars to buy gold from the United States Treasury and send the money home? They can always use that gold to settle up accounts with one another, but what can they do with dollars that far exceed their current needs?

Of course, foreigners have withdrawn substantial sums in the form of gold—our gold loss during the six years ended December 31, 1963 ran to nearly 7 billion dollars. But, as the increase in their dollar balances demonstrates, foreigners have been willing to accumulate their holdings of dollars at an even faster rate. In other words, much less than half of the deficit in our balance of payments has been covered by a loss of gold; much more than half has been covered by simply giving foreigners a *claim* on the gold (or anything else they want to buy from us) that they can exercise at any time they wish. Now, why has this been so?

Three factors account for these trends.

In the first place, the dollar has done a good job as an inexpensive substitute for gold. Since the United States has stood ready at all times to convert dollars into gold at $35 an ounce for foreign governments and central banks, and since our gold reserves relative to our demand liabilities to foreigners have been more than adequate,* the dollar in effect has been "good as gold." Holding assets in the form of gold is an expensive business in any case. It not only earns no interest, but is inflicted with a form of negative interest in that high fees have to be paid for its safekeeping, transfer, and shipment.

Second, it is an overstatement to assert that foreigners have had no use for the dollars that they have accumulated. They must carry substantial amounts of dollars simply to finance their day-to-day financial dealings with and purchases from Americans. Moreover, a large

* Britain served the same role as banker for the rest of the world for many decades on gold reserves that were only one fifth to one tenth the size of ours relative to the demand liabilities to foreigners outstanding against it. In any case, the United States has, in addition to its own gold reserves, substantial credits available to it from the International Monetary Fund.

and growing volume of business between foreigners is transacted in dollars rather than in sterling or francs or some other currency. This simple business reason is probably most important. In addition, however, many of these countries have been able to use the accumulation of excess dollars to make repayments on the money we lent them in the early postwar years, when they were desperately short of cash to pay for the enormous quantities of American goods and services so essential for the reconstruction of their economies.

Third, the monetary authorities have attempted to keep short-term interest rates in the United States sufficiently high to make foreigners want to hold dollar assets. During 1963, for example, the discount rate was raised from 3 to 3½ per cent. Free reserves were also allowed to run down from 0.4 million dollars at the beginning of the year to 0.1 million dollars at the end. With banks in a less liquid condition and preferring to liquidate short-term securities rather than to take the more expensive step of borrowing from the Federal Reserve to raise cash, the yield on U.S. Treasury bills rose from 2.9 per cent to 3.5 per cent during 1963.* More important than the absolute rise in rates, this shift narrowed the excessively wide gap that had previously stretched between interest rates in the United States

---

* The rise in short-term rates has had little effect on the interest rate on long-term obligations, which rose only 0.25 percentage points (as measured on Government securities) during 1963, compared with 0.60 percentage points on short-term bills. Because investors apparently believed that the influences playing on the United States balance of payments were temporary in nature, they were willing to commit funds for longer periods of time in the expectation that short-term rates might well go lower before the long-term bonds matured. They expected that, if they bought short- instead of long-term obligations, they would have to reinvest those sums at a lower rate of interest when the short-term obligation was paid off: they preferred the assurance of the prevailing rate over the life of the long-term obligation.

and other worldwide financial centers such as London, Paris, and Zurich.

Ultimately, however, the willingness of foreigners to hold dollars is more a compendium of hopes and fears than of cool economic calculations. Those countries with the largest claims on our gold—the Western Europeans and the Japanese—are also our strongest political allies; although they clearly enjoy some of our discomfiture over our present position, they would nevertheless want to avoid anything that would bring down in ruins the structure of international cooperation that has been built up during the postwar years. Each of them knows what a balance-of-payments crisis can be like; none of them would want us to be so angered that we would turn them down the next time they are in trouble. And, indeed, in time the balance-of-payments problem may well move across the oceans, for costs and prices in other industrial countries have for some years been rising very much faster than in the United States, with the result that their export-import balance has been growing less favorable while ours has become more so.

Yet the United States must clearly stop running deficits in its balance of international payments at some point. With our gold stock shrinking and the claims on it growing, we are in the precarious position of any banker who sees his cash resources draining away while his deposits are rising. At some point, there is going to be a run on his bank. What can be done to avoid it?

Many things are being done already. Expenditures for the maintenance of our military establishments abroad are being pared to the bone. Our foreign friends are being urged to make a larger contribution to Western defense and to the programs of assistance to underdeveloped countries. They have also been persuaded to convert some of their demand claims on the dollar into longer-term obligations of the United States Government, repayable in their own currencies.* Our interest rates have been raised to make holding dollars a more attractive business. The Government has worked hard to interest American businessmen in trying to sell more goods and services abroad. Steps have also been taken to try to persuade foreigners to raise less capital in the United States and to raise more from among themselves. Most hopeful—and most important, too—the trend toward higher prices and costs abroad is likely to persist for a long time.

But what really would happen if our position finally became untenable, despite all our efforts to stem the tide? At that unhappy moment, the United States would be forced to suspend convertibility of the dollar into gold.† The only way that foreigners could then dispose of their dollars would be to find someone else who wanted them—which, under those conditions, would mean that dollars would fall to a deeply depressed price in foreign exchange markets. In other words, whereas today an Englishman can obtain a dollar (or a dollar's worth of merchandise) for seven shillings and a Frenchman can obtain a dollar for five francs, they would then be able to swap perhaps as few as three or four shillings and two or three francs for one dollar. Conversely, of course, we would have to

---

* These are the so-called "Roosa bonds," named after the brilliant Undersecretary of the Treasury for Monetary Affairs, who accomplished so much in shoring up the defenses of the dollar.

† An even more distasteful step would be for the Government to take over and liquidate our assets abroad, using the proceeds to pay foreigners in their own money rather than in gold the sums they demand from us. But this would be even more politically and psychologically disastrous than breaking the tie with gold.

offer more dollars than we do today in order to obtain the same amount of their currencies.

In short, the dollar would be "devalued." Although this would help us out economically, in that foreigners would then find that they could buy more goods here with a smaller outlay of their own funds, the political and psychological consequences of this step could be disastrous. Foreigners holding dollars would have suffered grievous losses; few would trust our word again. Even if we were to return to free convertibility into gold, we would probably have to charge a much higher price for it than before in order to stretch out our shrunken gold supply—for example, foreigners might have to pay $50 for an ounce of gold compared with the current selling price of $35.* This is hardly the way to win friends and influence people; this is hardly the way for the world's richest and most powerful nation to behave.

Just because devaluation would be such a shocking blow to our prestige and power, and because it would at least disarrange and at worst disintegrate established patterns of trade and finance, the odds are heavily against its ever happening. But that is different from saying that it is impossible or that it is necessarily the worst choice among evils.

* The domestic impact of this development could also be significant. The Treasury's gold hoard would now be worth $50 an ounce instead of $35. In other words, the Treasury could print up additional gold certificates equal to the written-up value of the gold stock, deposit those gold certificates with the Federal Reserve Banks, and proceed to draw checks against those deposits. Thus, expenditures could be made without raising any money through taxing or borrowing. Both the reserves and the deposits of commercial banks would increase as a result, thereby increasing the likelihood of a major price inflation. However, devaluation of the dollar requires an act of Congress.

Indeed, without prejudging the issue, we can fairly state that men are excessively tenacious in clinging to established patterns, because, like Hamlet, they would rather "bear those ills we have/Than fly to others that we know not of." This is true of many things in our economy in addition to our attachment to gold at $35 an ounce.

Our analysis up to this point is sufficient to permit us to take a fresh look at some of these shibboleths. First, however, let us trace through some history to see how we got where we are, to see what has been done to help determine the movement of economic events in the fields of money, banking, and gold.

Part Five

THEORY IN PRACTICE

CHAPTER XIII

The Experience of 1938-45

How has all of this actually worked out in practice? Through what means and to what extent has the Federal Reserve System been able to regulate the supply of money and the pattern of interest rates? Even more important, what has been the effect of these movements in gold, in money, and in interest rates on the trend of economic conditions?

This chapter and the next survey the historical experience of the twenty-five year span from 1938 to 1963 in an effort to provide answers to these questions. We shall find four major segments within this period, each characterized by strikingly different economic forces and trends, and each demarcated from the other by a sharp and sudden shift in the fundamental environment. These separate segments cover the gold-rush years preceding World War II, the war years proper with their problems of war finance, the inflationary push from V-J Day to the Korean War, and the long period of rising interest rates, tightening money, and gold outflows that followed.

The story begins very differently from the way it ends. In the years preceding World War II, the American economy was characterized by widespread unemployment of both men and machines. Frightened Europeans were converting their capital into dollars, so that gold from abroad poured onto our shores and into the vaults at Fort Knox. The consequence was a mountainous rise in the reserves of commercial banks, from 7 billion dollars at the end of 1937 to 14 billion dollars three years later. But with relatively few credit-worthy borrowers around, and with interest rates at low levels, the banks were in no hurry to put their growing hoard of reserves to work, so that excess reserves also swelled from only a little more than 1 billion dollars to nearly 7 billion dollars over the same period of time.

Note that the expansion in excess reserves was smaller than the rise in total reserves. This shows that some increase in required reserves did take place, as a result of increased deposits in the commercial banks. Where did these increased deposits come from? In the first place, some growth in bank loans and investments did occur in response to the massive inflow of fresh reserves: investments went up about 6 billion dollars from

the end of 1937 to the end of 1940 as banks were
pressed to employ some of these idle resources, but it is
indicative of the depressed tone of business conditions
that loans at commercial banks hardly increased at all.
In addition, however, deposits at the banks increased
by an equal amount simply as a result of the gold inflow itself, as those who sold gold to the U.S. Treasury
deposited the proceeds in bank accounts in this country.

We know that interest rates reflect the interaction of
the demand for and supply of money. With business
activity rising so slowly, the need for cash to finance
expanding production during the 1930's was obviously
also growing at a slow rate. With ever-rising amounts of
money in the checking accounts of individuals and
corporations, those who held these idle dollars pressed
to find some employment for them. Long-term yields
on corporate bonds had been above 4 per cent when
Roosevelt took office in 1933; by 1938 they had fallen
to little more than 3 per cent and at Pearl Harbor were
down to only 2¾ per cent. At the same time, yields on
short-term paper, which had run well above 4 per cent
before the crash in 1929, fell to nearly zero.*

Yet, while the pattern of interest rates conformed to
the theoretical proposition that yields will go down
when the supply of money exceeds the demand for it,
the most striking feature of this period from our view-

* Another sign of the times was the widening spread between
the rate of interest on relatively riskless securities and on lower-
grade investments. In the late 1920's, bonds rated Aaa by
Moody's yielded about 4½ per cent, compared with about 5¼
per cent on bonds rated more risky, or Baa. By 1940, the yields on
the Aaa bonds had fallen to less than 3 per cent, while the Baa
bonds were still yielding more than 4 per cent. In other words, the
excess cash in the economy flowed much more readily into securities in which the credit risk was at a minimum.

point was really the degree to which the banks and their depositors were willing to hold dollars idle. Despite the avalanche of reserves that the gold rush brought to the banks, the banks were willing to lend and invest only a small part and were content to let cash resources in the billions sit idle, earning nothing. Even though the money supply rose about one third faster than the output of goods and services from 1933 to 1941, the decline in interest rates was persistent rather than precipitous. Finally, it was clear that the sheer pressure of funds was by no means a sufficient condition to drive business activity upward to its full potential—nobody's money seemed to be burning a hole in his pocket.

Monetary policy as a means of stimulating business activity fell into wide disrepute as a result of this combination of circumstances. Some people saw little point in efforts to increase the supply of money if no one wanted to spend those additional dollars on goods and services. What was the point in giving banks the resources to buy bonds that people wanted to sell, if the sellers just sat on the proceeds instead of spending them? Others argued that the banks were clearly unwilling to buy long-term bonds at low interest rates; therefore, no means existed to push interest rates down far enough to encourage businessmen to take the risks of borrowing and investing money in new factories to create new jobs.

Indeed, the fetish for liquidity during the 1930's was extraordinarily powerful—the simple creation of money (or receipt of money from abroad in the form of gold) was no guarantee that it would be spent. Some observers compared the stimulus of monetary policy with the effectiveness of pushing on a string. As a result, increasing interest and attention was focused on Government spending in excess of tax revenues—deficit financing, as it came to be called—in which the Government would borrow the idle dollars no one else wanted to use and spend them for things the community needed.

The arguments over the pros and cons of fiscal policy extend beyond the limits of this book. Whatever the shortcomings of the measures designed to overcome the economic and human disasters of the 1930's, there were some elements of good luck about the position in which we found ourselves when we entered the war at the end of 1941. Economically and financially, we were in excellent shape to mount the gigantic war effort that was called for.

For the economic impact of war is profound. Workers are taken away from the factories and the farms and turned into soldiers, thereby reducing the labor force available to produce goods and services. On top of that, the Government absorbs a substantial part of the country's total production, in order to sustain and equip the men on the battlefield. Unless a nation has a large reservoir of unemployed resources to throw into the war effort and unless its economy is highly productive, war inevitably forces on the civilian population a sharp reduction in living standards.

In addition, the war has to be financed; like any other spender in the economy, the Government has to find the money to pay for the things it wants to buy. Unless it literally prints the money, it will have to arrange to have the necessary funds transferred to it. But the methods of war finance, no matter what form they take, can do nothing to ease the real burden of the war effort, which is the diversion of production and manpower from the satisfaction of the needs of civilians to the provisioning of the machines of war. The techniques used to raise the money to pay for the war can significantly affect the *distribution* of that burden among different elements in the population, but it can do nothing to reduce it.

How did the U.S. Government find the almost incredible sum of 308 billion dollars that it spent on the war during the five years 1941-45?

The Government has one method of finance that is unique (although many people wish it were also available to them): the Government can *force* others to provide the money it needs. Taxation not only transfers purchasing power to the Government—it simultaneously reduces the amount of money available to the taxpayers to spend. In other words, the increase in the Government's purchasing power is exactly matched by the reduction in the taxpayer's purchasing power. Nothing makes more clear and dramatic the realities of the war effort—the forced diversion of purchasing power to the Government is a direct reflection of the forced diversion of manpower and production to the needs of war.

Of course, the Government could have financed our entire war effort through taxation. But politicians by temperament never want to make the harsh realities so clear as to finance a war entirely by taxation. Yet, in actuality, the repression of civilian living standards would have been no greater if they had.

But if the Government finds it politically impossible to raise taxes by such a large amount, then it must face the necessity of borrowing the difference. Borrowing, as we have seen, means inducing someone with excess cash on hand to part with that cash and to transfer it to someone else who has a use for it. However, this inducement commands a price. Furthermore, the more of these idle dollars the Government borrows and spends on the war effort, the fewer idle dollars are left—which means, in turn, that the interest rate the Government will have to pay will rise higher and higher as the borrowings increase.

The Treasury was faced with a serious dilemma at this point. Out of total budget expenditures of 340 billion dollars, 130 billion dollars were raised by taxation. The rest (some 210 billion dollars) had to be borrowed. But this enormous sum was five times greater than the total quantity of money held by the citizens and corporations and financial institutions in the United States in 1941. How, then, could the money be borrowed without sending interest rates to astronomical levels?* The remarkable fact is that the Treasury was borrowing money in the summer of 1945 just as cheaply as in the months preceding Pearl Harbor!

The answer, of course, is that the Treasury borrowed dollars that never existed before, that were held by no one until they came into the possession of the Treasury. There was no choice. If all the money could not be raised by taxation because of political obstacles, and if the remainder could not all be borrowed from holders of idle dollars because there were either insufficient idle dollars or because interest rates would have skyrocketed, then the necessary money had to be found elsewhere than in the taxpayer's pocket or in an inactive checking account.

In short, the Treasury borrowed about one-third of the money from the commercial banks. The checks the banks issued to pay for the Government bonds increased

* The chances are that there was too little money in the economy to accomplish this at any rate of interest. Therefore, prices would have had to be reduced drastically, so that a given number of dollars could finance the purchase of a large quantity of goods and services.

the Treasury's bank account without decreasing any other depositor's account. What the Treasury spent was new money, not a transfer to it of somebody else's money. Of course, when the Treasury spent that money, it moved into the pockets and bank accounts of the soldiers and sailors and armament producers and farmers, who, in turn, either spent it for their own needs or (as was frequently the case) checked it back to the Government again as money paid for taxes or money paid for Government bonds.

Out of total borrowings of 210 billion dollars from the end of 1940 to the end of 1945, 70 billion dollars were borrowed from the commercial banks. No wonder, then, that the war period was accompanied by a tremendous increase in the supply of money, from 40 billion dollars at the beginning to more than 100 billion dollars five years later. Since this was an even faster rate of expansion than the steep rise in the gross national product, more than enough money was created to finance the war effort. Thus, interest rates stayed at the low levels of the 1930's, even though Government debt more than quintupled.

If we think about it objectively, the ultimate impact on the economy would have been essentially the same if the Government had printed that 70 billion dollars instead of borrowing it from the commercial banks. Somewhere, the Government had to find this money that it either could not or would not raise from those who already had funds in their pockets and bank accounts. The money it created took no cash away from anybody and, in fact, increased the purchasing power of the civilian economy when it was spent by the Government. Isn't this exactly the same thing as printing new currency and paying it out to pay for the war? Times and forms change, but substance seldom does.

One final point is worth making here. Had the Government financed the war entirely by taxation or entirely by taxation and borrowing from lenders other than commercial banks, then individuals, corporations, and financial institutions would have had few dollars indeed to spend for any other purpose. With the available money supply so small, expenditures other than Government expenditures would have been extremely difficult to finance. Little danger of inflation would have existed under conditions of this nature, even though the supply of goods available to the civilian economy was also limited.

By financing part of the war effort through the creation of new money, however, the Government not only left purchasing power in the pockets of the civilian economy but, in fact, increased that purchasing power as it spent the new dollars provided by the commercial banks. The money supply burgeoned by more than 60 billion dollars, while the annual output of goods and services available for civilians to buy with it showed virtually no increase at all. A gigantic inflation would have resulted had we not had an intricate and bothersome network of price controls and rationing as a substitute for the normal allocating process of the price system.

How did the banking system finance these purchases of Government securities, and what role was played by the Federal Reserve during these years?

As the member banks had 7 billion dollars in excess reserves at the end of 1940, they clearly had ample resources to buy the Government bonds that began to be issued in such profusion. While the total volume of reserves held steady at around 13 to 14 billion dollars as the reserves lost by one bank when it bought a Govern-

ment bond were transferred to some other bank as the
Government spent the proceeds, the creation of new deposits resulting from the enormous purchases of Government bonds increased the volume of reserves the
banks were *required* to hold, so that required reserves
rose steadily and excess reserves were squeezed down
to only about 1 billion dollars.

But haven't we forgotten something from an earlier
chapter? What about the enormous outflow of currency
from the banks during the war years? Swollen by payments to soldiers and to farmers and by the use of currency in black market and tax-evading operations, currency in circulation rose from 8 billion dollars at the
end of 1940 to nearly 30 billion dollars by the end of
the war. As we have seen, these are withdrawals that
have no offsetting deposits and, therefore, drain reserves out of the banking system.

Consequently, the Federal Reserve Banks had to replenish the reserves the member banks lost through the
withdrawals of currency. Federal Reserve Bank purchases of Government securities during this period therefore amounted to 22 billion dollars—enough to offset
fully the loss of currency and to keep excess reserves
from falling below 1 billion dollars. This was, in fact,
another 22 billion dollars that the Government was
able to raise without tapping existing purchasing power.

The steadiness of interest rates during the war years
is a clear sign that the excessive amount of liquidity in
the American economy at the end of the Depression
was still there at the end of the war. The economy had
grown tremendously, the dollar volume of business activity was very much higher, the volume of outstanding
Government debt had reached levels no one could
have believed possible—but the money supply had ex-

panded fast enough to take care of all the additional financing that was necessary and keep interest rates at Depression levels as well.

During the war, of course, people were willing to put up with a lot for the sake of victory. Among other things, they tolerated without too much grumbling the rationing and price controls that were required to prevent our outsize money supply from causing a catastrophic inflation. Since taxation and direct borrowing had been insufficient to repress civilian demand, and since, in fact, our purchasing power had been increased as the Government spent the new dollars it borrowed from the banks, some mechanism had to be set up to keep the demand for civilian goods and services from racing too far ahead of the available supply.

But when the war was over, people wanted to use that money to buy the things they had been unable to find during the war and unable to afford during the Depression. Businessmen were restless to shake off the shackles of control. All the money built up as a result of the gold inflow of the 1930's and the subsequent impact of war finance rushed like a torrent into the postwar economy.

CHAPTER XIV

The Experience
of 1945-63

With the end of the war and the rapid dismantling of all wartime controls, the great pool of money that had formerly been flowing into the Treasury now burst upon the marketplace for automobiles, homes, clothes, appliances, butter, and meat for which people had been yearning for so long. But it was not only consumers who stampeded into the marketplace; businessmen were eager to re-equip their run-down productive facilities. Western Europe turned to us as well for assistance in the seemingly bottomless job of reconstruction, and countries that had prospered by staying out of the war also joined the queue of eager buyers.

The flow of expenditure was swollen by money that the Treasury returned to the rest of the economy. The war had come to an end at an early date that took the

Treasury by surprise, a large war loan having just been sold to the public during the spring of 1945. This extra cash, happily unnecessary for the war effort, was used to repay more than 20 billion dollars of Government debt during 1946 and 1947.

Whereas the physical output of goods and services in the early postwar years was probably a little lower, and surely no bigger, than it had been at the high point of war production in 1944 (although, of course, its composition changed competely), the demand for goods and services was so voracious that businessmen had no hesitation in taking advantage of the seller's market to raise prices. Workers, breaking out of the wartime wage-freeze, demanded and had little trouble in obtaining higher wages.

No problems of definition arose in describing the first three postwar years: this was inflation. Between the end of 1945 and 1948, consumer prices rose 33 per cent, and wholesale prices jumped a staggering 51 per cent. A good deal of this price stampede, however, was only a catching up to the inflationary pressures that had been generated during the war and dammed by price and rationing controls. From 1942 to 1945, for example, wholesale prices had risen by only 7 per cent.

Prices and wages were of course able to rise so fast because of the excess liquidity that had been accumulating ever since 1933. From 1933 to 1940, the money supply had expanded just slightly faster than the gross national product, but the potential increase in the money supply had been enormously swollen by the inflow of gold and consequent rise in the excess reserves of commercial banks. From 1940 to 1945, however, the money supply rose by two and a half times while gross national product just about doubled.

Furthermore, a large volume of money substitutes

had also been accumulated—assets so readily convertible into cash (such as savings deposits and U.S. Government Savings Bonds) that people were ready to spend their holdings of currency and money in checking accounts with the assurance that they could easily replenish their supply of money by cashing in these near-money liquid assets.

Without the accumulation of cash and liquid assets during the war years, the inflation of 1945-48 could never have taken place: no one could have afforded to pay the higher prices, no businessmen could have financed the rising cost of production. Naturally, some individuals and business firms had insufficient cash to finance all their expenditures. However, they had no difficulty in finding financial institutions eager to replace their low-yielding Government securities with more profitable investments. Credit was indeed abundant and remarkably easy to find.

The persistent liquidation of Government securities (or, what came to the same thing, the failure of holders of maturing Government bonds to replace them with new Government bonds) ran into substantial sums. From 1945 to 1950, commercial bank holdings of Government securities shrank by 30 billion dollars, while insurance companies and nonfinancial corporations liquidated on balance about 7 billion dollars more. Although individuals continued to accumulate Savings Bonds for a long time after the war, they nevertheless sold off nearly 4 billion dollars in marketable Government securities during the 1945-50 period.

As long as there was so much cash around, sellers of Government securities should have had no trouble in finding buyers. The difficulty was, however, that most investors were now looking for other types of assets that would provide a higher return. Furthermore, money that had been sitting during the war was now rapidly moving on the wing: the gross national product expanded by one third from 1945 to 1950 on an increase of only 10 per cent in the money supply. Another measure of the degree to which idle dollars were being put to active use is the sharp rise in debt among borrowers other than the Federal Government:

	Billions of dollars	
	1945	1950
State and local governments	13.7	20.7
Corporations	85.3	142.1
Individuals: farm	7.3	12.3
nonfarm	96.6	147.9
Total	202.9	323.0

These trends became the subject of profound concern. The economy had lived so long on low interest rates that low interest rates were considered a necessary condition for continued prosperity (especially in the construction industry). Any tendency toward higher interest rates thus appeared to be cause for alarm. Furthermore, aside from the pressures of the fundamental economic forces playing on the level of interest rates—the degree to which production was outpacing the supply of money—investor expectations also had to be considered. The fear arose that anticipation of higher interest rates would cause large-scale dumping of Government securities and that the millions of individuals who held more than 40 billion dollars in Savings Bonds redeemable on demand would rush to the Treasury and ask for their cash.

Once again, the Federal Reserve came to the rescue. While the Reserve Banks did let their shorter-term Government bonds run off by selling them or refraining from replacing them as they matured, they were heavy buyers of issues due in more than one year during the inflationary climax of 1948. Their holdings of these issues jumped from almost nothing to 12 billion dollars in twelve months. Consequently, the Federal Reserve successfully put its finger in the dike and staunched the flood of selling; the level of long-term interest rates was remarkably steady for a period characterized by such a powerful wave of economic expansion.

But the situation was reaching a critical point with the approach of 1950. Reserve Bank holdings of short-term securities had fallen so low that the Reserve Banks would soon have nothing to sell to offset their involuntary purchases of longer-term issues. If they were forced to stand ready to buy at pegged prices all Government securities offered for sale, in no matter what quantity, they would have had no means of limiting the supply of member bank reserves. In effect, they had lost control over the money supply at a time when inflation was rampant.

Although the Federal Reserve was dubbed an "engine of inflation," it performed the task with great reluctance. Relations between the officials of the System and the Truman administration were anything but cordial during this period. However, the impact of the Korean War during the summer of 1950 brought matters to a head. If another major and perhaps catastrophic wave of inflation were to be avoided under the pressures of war finance and renewed Federal deficits, the Federal Reserve had to be relieved of its obligation to be the residual buyer of Government securities offered for sale.

The result was what became known as the Treasury–Federal Reserve "Accord" of April 1951. The Federal Reserve naturally continued to be concerned that conditions in the Government securities market should be "orderly"—that is, that prices moved smoothly rather than discontinuously and that sufficient amounts were available to be bought or sold at various prices so that price changes would be gradual. But security prices were to be allowed to seek their own level, high or low. No longer was the Federal Reserve to be required to buy unlimited amounts of bonds at any price.

An entirely new set of relationships emerged during the post-Accord years. Federal Reserve policy, although flexible and willing to make credit readily available through the commercial banks during recessions, was nevertheless strongly biased in the direction of preventing further price inflation. The objective was to do everything possible to avoid a redundant money supply that would help to finance the persistent price increases of the 1950's. Although the dollar volume of business activity expanded by 75 per cent from 1951 to 1963, the supply of money in the form of demand deposits and currency increased by only 20 per cent. Consequently, the path of interest rates, despite brief interruptions during the periods of business recession, was clearly upward.

The real climax of this period came during the 13 per cent expansion in gross national product from 1958 to 1960 accompanied by less than a 3 per cent increase in the money supply. No wonder the interest yield on long-term bonds rose by nearly 50 per cent at that time, as business firms and individuals needing cash desperately strove to pry it loose from those who held it.

The view of this situation from the boardrooms of the commercial banks is reflected in the trends of the crucial magnitudes that determine banking policy— the supply of bank reserves available to finance an expansion in lending or in purchases of securities. And, despite the expansion in business activity, despite the rising demand for money to finance this expansion, the Federal Reserve refused to make additional reserves available to the commercial banks except on a temporary basis.

In other words, instead of buying Government securities in the open market and thereby providing a permanent addition to member bank reserves, the authorities insisted that the member banks come to the discount window and *borrow* the extra reserves they needed to meet the demand for credit. As a result, member bank borrowings from the Federal Reserve oscillated between virtually zero during recession periods to a level of 1 billion dollars or more during business expansions.

Once borrowings hit the 1-billion-dollar level—in 1952, in 1955-57, and again in 1959—banks became very strict indeed about granting new loans and tended to sell securities on balance. Then, a businessman or individual needing funds to finance a further rise in production or spending had to find a lender (or someone to buy the security he wanted to liquidate) outside the commercial banking system. It was in these years that interest rates consequently rose most steeply. Conversely, before the commercial banks would come back into the money and capital markets as buyers in sufficient volume to push interest rates downward again, they first reduced their indebtedness to the Federal Reserve well below the 1-billion-dollar level.

Now, however, let us turn our attention to another set of relationships that seems to contradict what we have just been discussing. For, although commercial bank holdings of Government securities moved up and down on a horizontal course from 1951 to 1963, loans made by member banks to business firms and to consumers showed a steep and virtually uninterrupted rise from about 50 billion dollars in 1951 to nearly 150 billion dollars by 1963!

How can it be that the banks were able to finance this enormous expansion in lending? Excess reserves in 1951 amounted to about 1 billion dollars, and we have seen that from time to time the banks borrowed up to approximately the same amount from the Federal Reserve, but these amounts are piddling next to the growth in their credit activities. Where did the banks find the necessary reserves?

The solution to this paradox lies in two developments —one planned, the other a by-product of a policy designed to achieve a different objective.

One reason why required reserves have risen so much more slowly than we might have expected is that the Federal Reserve authorities have reduced member bank reserve requirements in a series of steps as shown in the table below.

	Demand deposits			Time deposits
	Central reserve city banks*	Reserve city banks	Country banks	All banks
February 1, 1951	24%	20%	14%	6%
July 9, 1953	22	19	13	6
August 1, 1954	20	18	12	5
April 24, 1958	18	16½	11	5
September 1, 1960	17½	16½	12	5
December 1, 1960	16½	16½	12	5
November 1, 1962	16½	16½	12	4

* Formerly New York and Chicago; reclassified as reserve city banks on July 28, 1962.

In other words, a given volume of reserves has been able to support an increasing volume of commercial bank credit.

This policy was less a matter of choice than of necessity. There was no doubt that an expanding economy required additional sums of money to finance its growth. Whether the increase in the money supply should have been faster or slower was a matter of dispute, but everyone agreed that some increase in the quantity of money was called for to finance the growth in the economy. In order to provide the member banks with the reserves they needed to create this increased supply of money, the Federal Reserve would either have had to buy Government securities in the open market or lower member bank reserve requirements. One policy would have increased the total volume of reserves; the second would have permitted a given volume of reserves to support a larger amount of member bank loans and investments.

Now, we may recall that member bank reserves are to a major extent deposits in the Federal Reserve Banks. Under the law, the Federal Reserve is required to hold gold certificates equal to at least 25 per cent of those deposits. If the sums on the books of the Federal Reserve Banks to the credit of the member banks were to increase, then, of course, the amount of gold certificates held by the Reserve Banks would also have to increase. But, with the constant outflow of gold from the United States, the gold certificate reserve was shrinking, not rising. Thus, the Reserve authorities had no choice but to lower reserve requirements for member banks if they wanted the commercial banks to increase their loans and investments.

But another factor has also permitted a given volume of member bank reserves to support a larger level of deposits: this was also related to the tendency for foreigners to want to withdraw funds from the United States. For reasons that we have already explored in Chapter XII, the monetary authorities wanted to make it more attractive for foreigners to continue to hold balances in American banks. Consequently, in 1961, the maximum rate of interest that commercial banks were permitted to pay on time and savings deposits was increased significantly.

However the increase in rates offered by commercial banks on their time and savings deposits only intensified a trend that had already begun to manifest itself in the mid-1950's. Indeed, over 60 per cent of the expansion in total bank deposits since 1951 has been in time, rather than in demand, deposits. As the reserve requirement on time deposits is only one third to one quarter as much as on demand deposits, a much smaller volume of reserves has been necessary than would have been required if the public had chosen to hold more of its assets in the form of demand deposits.

Even though so much of the deposit expansion has been in time and savings accounts instead of checking accounts, what has happened has nevertheless been consistent with the process described in Chapter VI. While member bank loans and investments expanded by about 100 billion dollars from 1951 to 1963, total deposits in the member banks also increased by just about 100 billion dollars over the same period. The rise in member bank loans and investments, in other words, led to an equivalent increase in deposits, just as the theory predicts they would.

Nor does the pattern we see here mean that the commercial banks actually paid out the proceeds of loans or paid for securities they bought by creating new time deposits. The process that went on was precisely the same as the process described in Chapter VI: borrowers were paid by having sums added directly to their checking accounts at the bank where they borrowed the money, while sellers of securities were paid by checks that they deposited in their checking accounts at their own banks.

But obviously the public—which includes business firms and financial institutions other than commercial banks, as well as individuals—must have found that it was holding more of its assets in the form of checking accounts than it actually had to hold in that form. The attraction of high rates of interest on time and savings accounts induced businesses and individuals to cut down the balances in their checking accounts, on which they earned nothing, and to carry more in accounts on which they could earn interest. So long as the time and savings accounts were so readily convertible back into money, the public was willing to hold checking accounts down to a minimum working level. Thus, while the commercial banks now had to pay interest on deposits on which they formerly had had to pay nothing at all, they also could lend out and invest 96 cents of every dollar in time and savings accounts as compared with lending or investing only 80-odd cents of every dollar in demand deposits.

The shift of funds from demand to time deposits in commercial banks was one manifestation of an intricate and significant process that developed throughout the economy to the accompaniment of a generally rising trend of interest rates. As interest rates moved higher, the public sought a variety of ways to pick up some additional interest income on assets that, although not actually spendable money, were readily convertible into cash. What we find, as a result, is that the total of savings accounts of various types plus holdings of short-term Treasury securities and other forms of short-term obligations expanded rapidly from less than 300 billion dollars in 1951 to nearly 500 billion dollars in 1963. In contrast, money in the form of demand deposits and currency rose only from 123 to 153 billion dollars over the same period.

In effect, new techniques have evolved to mobilize our available money supply by making it unattractive and expensive to hold money idle. The lure of higher interest rates has encouraged people to find ways to put their money to work, and that in turn has made it easier for those who need cash to borrow it or to find buyers for the assets they choose to liquidate.

But these changing attitudes toward money and "near-money" liquid assets can lead to unexpected consequences. The advantage of holding a liquid asset other than money is in the interest return it provides, together with the assurance that it can be readily converted back into cash at little or no risk. But what if everyone wants cash at the same time? We can't all be taking money in while none of us wants to pay it out. A liquid asset is "liquid" only so long as other people have cash they would be willing to part with in exchange for it.

Think, too, of the consequences to the commercial banks if people decide to spend the money they had previously let lie in a time deposit collecting interest. Banks have to hold in reserve against demand deposits three to four times as much as they have to hold against time deposits. Thus, a shift from time to demand deposits at the end of 1963 of only those sums that had gone into time deposits during the three preceding years would have required the member banks to hold in reserve 15 per cent more than they were actually holding. The banks would then have to stop making new loans and would be heavy sellers of securities: if they drew money away from the public, the liquidity squeeze in the economy would become even more in-tense.

These trends have had another curious corollary. Whereas the public has been feeling more liquid, the banks have actually been moving into an increasingly illiquid condition. This partly reflects sufficient confi-dence on the part of bank officers that the American economy is now so stable that wholesale withdrawals of cash from the banking system, as happened in the 1930's, are highly unlikely. But it also reflects the belief of bankers that most of the money in time deposits will stay there instead of moving into demand deposits where the odds are much greater that it will soon be withdrawn. This is reflected in the declining share of U.S. Government securities, the most liquid of all earning assets, as a percentage of total commercial bank loans and investments, from 59 per cent in 1947 to 31 per cent in 1961 and to only 26 per cent at the end of 1963.

Of course, none of these trends need lead to difficulty so long as current patterns prevail. They suggest, how-ever, that a reversal of current patterns, prompted, per-haps, by a rising demand for money occasioned by an inflationary cycle, could ultimately cause a monetary crisis as intense as anything witnessed in our earlier history.

Meanwhile, however, the substitution of liquid assets for money seems to be a process with strong forward momentum. And it has once again raised questions about the effectiveness of monetary policy in controlling the economy. We may recall that monetary policy was in disrepute during the 1930's because simply increasing the supply of money seemed only to create idle dollars instead of money that people wanted to lend or spend; it satisfied the demand for liquidity but did nothing to stimulate the demand for goods and services. Now the opposite question has been raised: if in prosperous times the demand for liquidity is so easily satisfied and if the proliferation of substitutes for money permits a given supply of money to finance a rising level of business activity, how can the monetary authorities prevent an inflation merely by limiting the supply of money as such?

As a result, the focus of attention has been shifting from the supply of money to the supply of credit, from the actual cash holdings of the public to the institutional arrangements that facilitate the task of those requiring financing to find it. Within this framework, the regulation of the supply of money appears to be only part of the broader problem of the use of money or the flow of expenditure. Proponents of this view urge a wide extension of the responsibilities of the Federal Reserve authorities to include both specific controls over credit, such as setting maximum loan terms on consumer or mortgage credit and control over the lending and investing activities of the "financial intermediaries" —the savings banks, savings and loan associations, finance companies, insurance companies, and even the money market itself.

Other observers believe that the old theory is still valid—that there are still limits to how far business activity can advance without an increase in the supply of money. Although, admittedly, the rising interest rates of the 1950's did encourage the development of institutional arrangements that helped those seeking cash to find it and did increase the attractiveness of holding near-money assets that brought an income, these adjustments may well have run their course. After all, currency and checking accounts are still the only things we use to buy things with and to pay our debts. Business cannot expand indefinitely on credit: purchases ultimately have to be paid for, and paid for with money. If we are to limit the supply of credit, we must begin by limiting the supply of money.

But this brings us to the final questions we must ask. How far should we go, and to what purpose, in limiting the supply of money? Is the danger of inflation so persistent in the American economy and the threat to our gold stock so serious that monetary policy must continue to be tilted in the direction of holding down rather than giving free rein to the expansion in purchasing power? These are the subjects of our final section.

CONCLUSION

Money and Gold in the Future

When Lenin predicted that the Soviets would some day use gold to coat the walls and floors of their public lavatories, he was expressing his scorn for the tyranny of money. But this attitude has been no monopoly of the Communists. It echoed the famous words of William Jennings Bryan: "You shall not crucify mankind upon a cross of gold." Indeed, reformers and advocates of social change have long been in conflict with the more conservative supporters of "sound money," in a tradition that began before Andrew Jackson and runs through to the present day.

It is curious that this should be so, for conservatives are just as interested as anyone else in seeing the country prosperous and fully employed. Nevertheless, the man who lends money wants to be sure that the money he receives in repayment will buy as much as the cash he originally parted with; he knows that when credit is too easy to obtain, demand outruns supply, prices tend to rise, and money loses its value. Conservatives also believe that progress should come slowly, with plenty of time for trial and error, in order to avoid excesses and distortions that may lead to disaster. They know that providing too much money too fast will permit the financing of too many projects doomed to fail the inexorable tests of profitability.

The controversy has lost none of its intensity with the passage of time. Today those who warn most vigorously against the dangers of inflation are the same people who insist that gold is the only satisfactory basic means of payment among nations. On both scores, they are skeptical about the ability of men to show the self-control and moderation that would be required if legal and natural restrictions on the quantity of money were to be removed. But they are confronted with other men who are impatient with barriers to expansion that seem arbitrary in origin and that have been accompanied by chronic unemployment and underutilization of productive capacity.

Let us explore briefly this second and less orthodox view of the management of money and gold—not because of any desire to take sides, but rather because the accepted doctrine receives so much more attention and so thoroughly dominates the pages of the financial press. Only in books and journals written for professional economists (where the presentation tends to be pedantic and complex) or in the works of biased popular writers (where the case is badly argued) does any irreverence or any doubt appear concerning the conventional wisdom that inflation is our greatest enemy and that gold must continue to be the ultimate determinant of our economic fate.

In any case, a primer on money and gold should properly ask whether inflation is as great a threat to the American economy as it is supposed to be—and, even if it is, whether monetary policy is adequately equipped to restrain it.

Indeed, the long-run history of prices in the United States denies the myth of permanent inflation. Although we have never had a war without an inflation, our peacetime price record appears as a horizontal oscillation, with at least as many years of declining prices as years of so-called inflation.

There is no mystery why this should be so. The American economy is fabulously productive and intensely profit-oriented. When demand exceeds supply and buyers are willing to spend more money for the same quantity of goods, profits expand. This expansion attracts fresh capital and savings and induces existing producers to expand their production. Before long, supply has caught up with demand and prices begin to recede again. The remarkable aspect of the price inflation that broke out immediately after World War II was not its magnitude—pent-up demands were enormous and the quantity of money available to finance them was much more than adequate—but, rather, its brevity. Within three years after V-J Day most shortages had been overcome and prices began to decline. Excluding the impact of the Korean War, the average annual rise in the cost of living in the years 1948-63 was little more than 1 per cent a year and only half that rate in wholesale prices. This is surely too little to have much influence on people's decisions to spend or to save.*

But isn't there a danger that acceptance of the inevitability of inflation and, in particular, a relaxation of the anti-inflationary bias of monetary policy could in fact lead people to buy in advance of their needs and to abandon their holdings of bonds, life insurance, and savings accounts?

This possibility does exist. But one can find little or no evidence that it is likely to happen. According to one major and authoritative study of this subject,† truly radical shifts in savings patterns and in people's willingness to hold cash do not start until prices have at least doubled in six months or less. In many countries, inflationary price rises of 10 to 15 per cent a year have persisted without causing a breakdown of the country's financial system.

When all is said and done, the productivity of the American economy is the ultimate barrier to runaway inflation in our country. The catastrophic inflations of history—and many large, but less disruptive, infla-

---

* Inflation has been a dominating topic of conversation in the stock market for many years and probably a majority of investors believe they are buying common stocks as a hedge against inflation. From a rational viewpoint this has made little sense: supposedly poor inflation hedges such as utilities, railroads, and food processors have been far better holdings than the traditional hedges such as metals and mining companies, real estate syndicates, and crude oil producers. Furthermore, prices of common stocks (as measured by Standard & Poor's 500) have risen five times as fast as the cost of living since the end of World War II, so that hedging against inflation must have been only one of many motivations to buy and hold common stocks.

† Brown, A. J., *The Great Inflation* (New York: Oxford University Press, 1955), p. 195. See also Scitovsky, T. and A., "Inflation and Unemployment: An Examination of their Effects," in Conard, J. *et al.*, *Inflation, Growth, and Employment*, Commission on Money and Credit (Englewood Cliffs, N.J.: Prentice-Hall, Inc., 1964), pp. 429–470.

tions—have been the result of a real shortage of goods and a breakdown of the economy's ability to produce and distribute, rather than of an excess of money. This was clearly the case in the Confederacy during the Civil War, and in the defeated countries of Europe and Asia after World War I and World War II. It has also been the case in the underdeveloped nations, where resources must be devoted to building roads and factories and power plants rather than to consumer goods while at the same time the demand for consumer goods is burgeoning. These types of problems simply do not exist in the American economy (or exist only mildly and very briefly, as in 1955-57), where, for most of the peacetime years in the twentieth century, our capacity to produce has exceeded our willingness to buy.

But even if we can avoid the most serious forms of inflation, isn't even a little inflation a bad thing? Even if the habits of consumers remain unchanged despite gradually rising prices, aren't businessmen likely to accumulate excessive amounts of inventory and to expand plant and equipment far beyond their immediate needs, in order to hedge against higher prices in the future? And doesn't this ultimately lead to falling production and to rising unemployment when the inventories are bulging out of the warehouses and when productive capacity is clearly out of line with the demands of customers? Doesn't the rising cost of living make workers press for higher wages that then squeeze profits and consequently cause business to cut back production and employment?

Yes, these patterns are most typical in our type of economy and do indeed describe the greatest difficulties likely to develop if we drop our guard against an outbreak of inflation. But it is also fair to ask whether the cure may be worse than the disease: are the conse-

quences of trying to avoid inflation any less serious
than the consequences of the mild form of inflation
that we typically experience?

First of all, we are faced with the extraordinarily difficult problem of choosing exactly the right set of policies
at exactly the right moment. In an economy as enormous, diversified, and complex as ours, who is to determine the precise level of demand sufficient to keep
industry humming but not so great that it exceeds the
quantity of goods and services we can produce?

If the economy is sufficiently liquid so that financing
of expenditures is possible without the assistance of the
commercial banks, monetary policy will be hard put to
stop inflation in any case. If, on the other hand, financing is made so difficult that expenditures fall short of
the desired level, men will be unemployed and machines will stand idle. This is especially likely if, as
usually happens, prices and wages refuse to come down
in the face of shrinking demand. In addition, we have
no assurance that demand will be restricted in just those
spots where it is excessive—it does no good to deny
credit to the corner grocery store when large corporations accumulating raw materials are able to get all the
credit they need.

Most important, the dangers inherent in too little
demand may be greater than the dangers of too much.
If business firms are operating below their full potential, we lose many of the economies of high-volume production. Instead of a risk-taking, enterprising economy
running under a full head of steam, with production
moving to ever higher levels and new products and new
techniques the order of the day, we have an economy
strangled in the rigidities and insecurities of an inadequate level of demand. Labor fights against automation
and other types of progress that would improve pro-

ductivity. Minority groups feel the impact of job discrimination even more intensely than usual. Overhead costs, spread over a smaller rather than a larger number of units of output, loom high and cut into profit margins. Finally, the evidence suggests that at least 6 per cent (and probably a larger proportion) of the labor force must be unemployed if wage increases are to be kept in check—and this is a politically and socially intolerable level of unemployment.

Perhaps most significant, no data exist to prove that countries with relatively stable price levels show faster rates of economic growth than countries with rising price levels. A country-by-country analysis of postwar experience throughout the world shows cases in which inflation was accompanied by rapid growth and others in which it was accompanied by slow growth. It also shows both slow and rapid growth associated with cases in which prices were relatively stable.

For example, of the countries of Western Europe, only West Germany and Belgium had a smaller increase in living costs than the United States had during the decade of the 1950's, but Belgium's rate of economic growth was below ours and West Germany's was much above. Austria and the United Kingdom showed the greatest increases in living costs; Austria's rate of growth was second only to Germany's, whereas Britain's growth rate was the slowest of all. Denmark and France showed the same rise in living costs, but France's output expanded nearly twice as fast as Denmark's.

In short, we have no basis for believing that stable prices are essential for economic growth and full employment, nor can we necessarily argue that, in the difficult business of matching demand to supply, we would do better to err on the side of too little demand than on the side of too much.

.   .   .

But what about the gold? Perhaps one could make the case that both the dangers and the consequences of inflation have been overstated, but don't we still have to protect the dollar internationally? If pursuit of our domestic objectives requires us to abandon our external obligations, which alternative should we choose?

Although the arguments we have just reviewed indicate that inflation may be less of a problem in practice than the theoretical position against it might suggest, the practical case for defending our gold stock and the international status of the dollar is stronger than the theoretical one.

For the theoretical one stands on rather weak ground. In the first place, sacrificing anything for the sake of gold seems hardly rational. Sacrifices in order to have more houses or more factories or more roads or even more foreign investments or more atom bombs make some sense. Each of these has some use or serves some purpose. But gold in and of itself is useless: that is the whole point of the Midas legend. The Russians, for example, may some day want to coat their public conveniences with gold, but surely they are better off in the meantime to ship the gold out and to bring wheat in.

While most nations hold dollars in preference to gold as part of their foreign exchange reserve against a rainy day, the United States accrues relatively little bread-and-butter advantage from this position as a "key currency." The willingness of foreigners to accumulate dollars has indeed enabled us to pay out to them more than they have paid over to us, but their continued preference for holding dollars has required us to protect the purchasing power of the dollar through excessive levels of unemployment and less-than-maximum rates of growth in our levels of production.* Giving up our position as a key currency would also involve certain economic costs, but they might well turn out to be smaller than the costs of preserving it.

In any case, why should the patterns of international trade be ruled by the arbitrary limits that nature has set on the supply of gold? Some experts have argued for the creation of a new international currency to replace or supplement gold, to be expanded and contracted as needed under the direction of an international central bank similar in character to our own domestic Federal Reserve Banks. Although as a practical matter, such an arrangement would require an extraordinary amount of international coordination and cooperation—to say nothing of the familiar and inescapable problem of keeping the supply of international purchasing power neither too low nor too high—no theoretical argument against it can be made.

But, no, the practical and political difficulties in the way of abandoning gold seem insurmountable. As in the past, we can continue to chip away at the golden foundations on which our domestic and international financial relationships have been built, but we shall have to restrain our theoretical impatience for the sake of our practical obligations. It is not the international financial position of the *dollar* that is our basis for concern here: the international prestige and position of the American people is at stake. Similarly, on a domestic level, no matter how strong the theoretical case that one can make, recognition of people's primitive and visceral responses to money matters must be taken

* Conceivably these restrictive policies may have *damaged* rather than helped our balance of payments, by discouraging foreign investment in the United States and encouraging American investment abroad.

into consideration. Habits of using and of thinking about money run deep and change with agonizing slowness.

The purpose of this book, in fact, has been to speed up, if only a little, the understanding of the nature and use of money, to broaden the reader's horizon to the point where he will at least consider ideas that he might otherwise have rejected outright. But perhaps the purpose goes further than that. To return to the point from which we started: money and gold have no use or value in themselves. On the contrary, *their value derives only from what we can buy with them.*

In short, our wealth lies neither in the vaults at Fort Knox nor on the ledgers of our banks. Rather, it lies all around us, in what we have so prodigiously produced in the past and what we are capable of producing in the future.

APPENDIX

Reading the
Weekly Federal Reserve
Statement

Central bankers by temperament tend to be taciturn. Since many of their decisions can have a major impact on the trend of security prices and, ultimately, on business activity, they want to do as little as possible to encourage speculation among investors and business executives in anticipation of change in central bank policy. This is not just because speculation usually feeds on itself and inevitably increases instability in the economy. To the extent that speculation goes on, it complicates their job by obscuring the basic economic trends that the central bank authorities are attempting to influence in one direction or the other.

If most of the deliberations of the directors of the twelve Federal Reserve Banks, of the Board of Gover-

nors of the System, and of the Open Market Committee in Washington are in secret, is there any way that
we can follow the direction and intensity of Federal Reserve policy?

Although changes in the discount rate or in reserve
requirements are obvious signs of Federal Reserve intentions, a careful reading of the Federal Reserve
Banks' weekly statements can yield useful clues and
keep the astute observer up on trends in monetary policy. Indeed, reading this statement each week is one of
the great detective games in the financial world, as the
effort is made to sift normal operating procedures or
random variations in the data from intended changes
prompted by policy decisions on the part of the authorities.

As we have already seen, the fulcrum of monetary
policy is the supply of member bank reserves relative to
the quantity of reserves that the banks are required to
hold against their deposits. As the Federal Reserve
authorities have no direct control over the volume of
deposits in member banks, and as they are reluctant to
change the percentage reserve requirement (except at
widely separated intervals), their only means of influencing the member banks to increase or reduce their
loans and investments is by causing changes to occur
in the total quantity of member bank reserves. Even
here, their controls are somewhat limited, as member
banks borrow reserves or repay borrowings at the Federal Reserve on their own initiative. Nevertheless,
through the tool of open-market operations—the purchase and sale of Government securities by the Federal
Reserve Banks—the authorities have a powerful technique for causing changes in the supply of member
bank reserve balances.

Complications arise, however, because many extraneous factors also cause member bank reserves to vary. An increased demand for currency by the public, the inflow of gold to the United States, and delays in the clearing and collection of checks are examples of events that affect member bank reserves and over which the Reserve authorities have no control. Therefore, in order to avoid erratic and excessive swings in the size of bank reserves from day to day, or even from month to month, a substantial part of Federal Reserve open-market operations will have nothing whatsoever to do with monetary policy but will be designed purely as steps to offset these seasonal or happenstance variations in other factors that are causing member bank reserves to vary. Finally, of course, the volume of reserves the banks are required to hold will vary with the level of deposits (and the mix between demand and time deposits), and this figure can also swing widely as a result of seasonal or erratic influences.

One can follow all of these procedures regularly in each Friday morning's newspaper, which shows the balance sheet of the Federal Reserve Banks as of the close of business on the preceding Wednesday. The newspaper will also show a separate table, combining and rearranging the figures from the bank balance sheets, that help the reader to follow the major elements of the situation. To make matters as simple as possible, the usual exceedingly wide daily variations are eliminated in this separate table, through the device of showing the *average* of the daily figures for the week ending with the preceding Wednesday. The average figures for the preceding week and for the same week of the preceding year are also shown for purposes of comparison.

.   .   .

Before looking at an actual statement and seeing how we might analyze it, let us first list briefly the various items that appear in this statement, with an explanation of the manner in which they cause changes to occur in member bank reserves.

The table begins by showing Federal Reserve open-market operations: *purchases or sales of Government securities* and *repurchase agreements.* The latter cover arrangements that the Reserve Banks make with Government security dealers to buy from them temporarily certain amounts of Government securities, on the condition that the dealers will repurchase the securities at a specified date and at a specified price. In other words, repurchase agreements are really short-term loans made by the Reserve Banks to the Government security market.

The table then shows *discounts and advances to member banks,* which reveals the extent to which the member banks are borrowing reserves or repaying their debts at the Reserve Banks.

The next item, called *float,* conventionally appears within the grouping summed up as Federal Reserve Credit. Float arises as the result of delays in the clearing of checks through the commercial banking system. For example, a man in New York receives a check from a customer in San Francisco. He deposits that check in his local bank, which in turn deposits it at the Federal Reserve Bank of New York. Neither he nor his bank can use that money until enough time has elapsed for the check to have returned to the local commercial bank in San Francisco against which it was drawn, after passing through the Federal Reserve Bank of San Francisco. If, however, owing to weather or other delays, the check takes longer than expected to get back to the bank against which it was drawn, the Reserve authorities will nevertheless allow the depositor and his local bank in New York to have the use of that money. As accounts have been credited in New York, but no one's account in San Francisco has yet been reduced, the people in New York *and* in San Francisco have the use of that money until the check finally does clear.

Float usually runs around 1 billion dollars. It will vary with the character of the weather (especially in winter), with strikes and other factors that could delay the movement of the mails, and, of course, with the volume of checks in process. The volume of checks in process usually hits a peak around the middle of the month, when most companies pay their bills, and then tapers off toward the end of the month. While this seems like a complicated and unnecessarily messy factor, a float of a billion dollars or so is negligible compared with weekly check clearings that average nearly 100 billion dollars a week.

We analyzed the effect of changes in the *gold stock* on member bank reserves in Chapter XI. Increases in the gold stock permit the Treasury to deposit gold certificates in the Federal Reserve Banks and to spend the proceeds, thereby increasing member bank reserves. Decreases in the gold stock have the opposite effect.

Treasury currency outstanding refers to that part of our currency and coin that is issued by the Treasury rather than by the Federal Reserve. It consists largely of silver certificates and coin. Its impact on member bank reserves is precisely the same as the impact of the issuance of gold certificates—it gives the Treasury money to spend that will move into member bank reserves as the Treasury disburses the funds it has deposited in this manner at the Federal Reserve.

Currency in circulation refers to all currency and coin held outside the Federal Reserve Banks. In other words, it covers currency and coin in the hands of the public and of business firms, together with the currency and coin held in the vaults of the commercial banks. An increase in currency in circulation reduces member bank reserves on deposit at the Federal Reserve, as the banks must withdraw the currency they need from the Federal Reserve Banks. A reduction in currency in circulation permits the commercial banks to redeposit the currency in their accounts at the Federal Reserve. To the extent that banks increase their holdings of vault cash, which count as legal reserves against deposits, an increase in currency in circulation is offset by the rise in vault cash in figuring the impact on *total* member bank reserves, and vice versa.

Deposits, other than member bank reserves, held with Federal Reserve Banks, include accounts carried at the Federal Reserve Banks by the U.S. Treasury, by foreign governments and foreign central banks, and by nonmember commercial banks which are permitted to carry such accounts for clearing purposes under certain circumstances. Checks drawn against such accounts will be deposited by their payees in commercial banks, which will in turn deposit those checks in their Federal Reserve accounts. Thus, withdrawals from these "other than member bank reserves" accounts tend to increase member bank reserves, and vice-versa.

Treasury cash covers cash assets held by the Treasury other than those on deposit at the Federal Reserve. The largest part of Treasury cash consists of gold held by the Treasury against which no gold certificates were ever issued. If the Treasury were to issue such gold certificates and deposit them at the Federal Reserve, Treasury cash would go down, but the impact on member bank reserves would be the same as if the gold stock had gone up. On the other hand, if the Treasury buys gold and issues no gold certificates against it, Treasury cash goes up, but the Treasury will have to tax or borrow the money to pay for the gold, so that member bank reserves would tend to go down.

Now, how does all of this help us to obtain a better picture of how the Federal Reserve actually operates?

Here is what these various factors looked like during the week ending September 25, 1963:

Averages of Daily Figures*
(millions of dollars)

		9/25/63	Change from: 9/18/63	9/26/62
Factors supplying reserves				
1. Fed. Res. holdings of Govt. securities				
2.	Bought outright	32,040	−169	+2,700
3.	Repurchase agreements	—o—	—o—	—o—
4.	Total	32,040	−169	+2,700
5. Discounts and advances to member banks		418	+193	+ 266
6. Float		1,937	− 58	− 239
7. Total Fed. Res. credit		34,434	− 34	+2,732
8. Gold stock		15,582	—o—	− 486
9. Treasury currency outstanding		5,587	− 3	+ 39
10. *Total factors supplying reserves*		55,603	− 37	+2,285
Factors absorbing reserves				
11. Currency in circulation		35,850	−166	+1,968

* Totals may not add due to rounding. Line 7 also includes some minor miscellaneous credit granted to other than member banks.

12.	Deposits, other than member bank reserves, with Fed. Res. Banks			
13.	Treasury	856	− 86	+ 362
14.	Foreign	139	− 3	− 80
15.	Other	181	− 28	− 102
16.	Treasury cash	385	− 37	− 16
17.	Other Federal Reserve accounts	1,140	− 1	+ 380
18.	*Total factors absorbing reserves*	38,551	−319	+2,512
	Member bank reserves			
19.	With Federal Reserve Banks*	17,052	+282	− 226
20.	Currency and coin in vaults	3,148	+ 18	+ 235
21.	Total member bank reserves	20,200	+300	+ 9
22.	Required	19,740	+188	+ 53
23.	Excess (Total less required reserves)	460	+112	− 44
24.	Free (Excess reserves less borrowings)	42	− 81	− 310

* This figure will always be the difference between the total of factors supplying reserves (line 10) less the total of factors absorbing reserves (line 18).

The best way to begin to look at the statement is by noting the direction of the changes in those non-policy factors that are likely to be large and erratic—particularly the change in the float (line 6), in currency in circulation (line 11), in the Treasury account at the Federal Reserve (line 13), and in required reserves of member banks (line 22). In this particular week, the float was running off as the large volume of mid-month checks was finally being cleared, currency in circulation declined as Labor Day currency withdrawals gradually returned to the banks, the Treasury was paying out somewhat more money than it was taking in, and member bank required reserves showed a sharp upward jump, probably reflecting an increase in deposits associated with an expansion in loans to finance the usual seasonal autumn rise in business activity. The net impact of these four factors on member bank reserves was substantially to offset one another, so that on balance they had no significant effect at all that week.

Note, however, that the Reserve Banks were selling Government securities during the week (line 2), thereby reducing member bank reserves at a time when the autumn rise in business activity was pushing required reserves upward (line 22). No wonder, then, that the banks had to borrow back (line 5) the reserves they were losing as a result of Federal Reserve open-market operations. Although the return of currency from circulation and the net disbursements by the Treasury did tend to raise member bank reserves, excess reserves (line 23) increased by a much smaller amount than the amount the banks felt they had to borrow. Consequently, free reserves (line 24) dropped off sharply.

In short, these figures tell quite a story. The Federal Reserve made clear its intention to supply only grudgingly the reserves required by the banks to finance the rising level of business activity. This meant that money would be somewhat more difficult and more expensive to obtain. It also suggested that the commercial banks would be forced to sell securities if they wanted to expand their loans to business firms and consumers.

If we look at the trend of developments over a period of a year, we can see at once that the Federal Reserve Banks were heavy buyers of Government securities (line 2). On closer examination, however, Federal Reserve purchases of Government securities provided little more in the way of reserves to the member banks than to offset the loss of reserves caused by an expansion in currency in circulation (line 11)—a natural accompaniment of increasing production and employment —and the loss of gold to foreign countries (line 8). Indeed, had the member banks been less willing to borrow additional reserves (line 5), they would never have been able to increase their own loans and Government security holdings to the extent that they did, as indicated by the rise in their required reserves (line 22). It is clear that money was more difficult and expensive to obtain in the latter part of 1963 than it had been in 1962.

Thus, careful study of the weekly Federal Reserve statement is an essential part of following fundamental trends in monetary policy and, in fact, in those aspects of money, banking, and gold that influence and are influenced by the tempo of general economic conditions.

BIBLIOGRAPHY

The subject of money, banking, and gold is so important and its content has changed so much over time, that the temptation to create a bibliography running into hundreds of titles is difficult to resist. However, the purpose of this bibliography is to mention the reading material that covers the essentials of the subject and the areas of most interest and controversy that surround it.

Five volumes are basic to an understanding of money, banking, and gold beyond the level touched by this book.

The serious student should surely read *The General Theory of Employment, Interest, and Money* by John Maynard Keynes (New York: Harcourt, Brace & World, Inc.), unquestionably the most important book in economics written in our century. Particular attention should be given to Chapters XIII-XV, which discuss specifically the relationships among the supply of money, the level of interest rates, and the trend of business activity.

A volume published more than forty years ago has never lost its freshness, its insights, and its eloquence. *Money,* by the English economist D. H. Robertson (New York: Harcourt, Brace & World, Inc.), is truly an extraordinarily perceptive and illuminating work.

Another book old in years but of immense importance for the understanding of central banking and money markets is *Lombard Street,* by the famous nineteenth-century economist Walter Bagehot (London: Kegan Paul, Trench, Trubner & Co., Ltd.).

The most recent important book in the field is *A Monetary History of the United States, 1867-1960,* by Milton Friedman and Anna J. Schwartz (New York: The National Bureau of Economic Research). This highly controversial work takes the position that money is the primary determinant of business activity and employment, that the monetary authorities have done a poor job of regulating the supply of money, and that we should automatically permit an increase of 3 to 4 per cent per annum in the money supply in order to assure an adequate rate of economic growth. Whether one subscribes to this approach or not, the book is a gold mine of fascinating statistics and highly stimulating argument and analysis.

Finally, Lawrence Ritter's excellent book of readings, *Money and Economic Activity* (Boston: Houghton Mifflin Co.), second edition, contains a collection of the major articles from professional journals on this subject in recent years. Aside from the Friedman approach, the other major area of controversy has been the Gurley-Shaw thesis that financial institutions other than the commercial banks have so effectively mobilized the money supply that simply controlling the quantity of money in the form of demand deposits is inadequate to the task of influencing the rate of expenditure in the economy. This is well covered in Ritter's *Readings,* together with authoritative and thorough discussions of the other topics touched upon in these pages.

The Commission on Money and Credit volume, *Inflation, Growth, and Employment,* by Joseph W. Conard *et al.* (Englewood Cliffs, N.J.: Prentice-Hall, Inc.) covers in great detail most of the theories of inflation, the effectiveness of the various types of inflation controls, and the relationships among inflation, employment, and economic growth. The book is well documented with excellent statistical material.

Federal Reserve Policy Reappraised, 1951-1959, by David S. Ahearn (New York: Columbia University Press) is an unusually interesting and informative discussion and criticism of the tools of Federal Reserve control and the manner in which they have been used.

The Federal Reserve System publishes important material relating to the subject. Most of the relevant current statistics appear in the monthly *Federal Reserve Bulletin* and in the *Federal Reserve Chartbook,* published by the Board of Governors in Washington. Each of the twelve Federal Reserve Banks also publishes interesting monthly letters that are free. In addition, the Board of Governors has published a useful little volume, also free, *The Federal Reserve System: Its Purposes and Functions* (latest edition, 1963), that makes an excellent elementary introduction to the subject. A number of the Federal Reserve Banks have also published volumes on the operation of the System and the role of money in our economy. Of these, the most important and useful is *Federal Reserve Operations in the Money and Government Securities Markets,* by Robert V. Roosa (Federal Reserve Bank of New York).

The literature on gold and the U.S. balance of payments is of course voluminous. The two most interesting and informative, albeit controversial, works on the current aspects of the gold crisis are *Gold and the Dollar Crisis,* by Robert Triffin (New Haven: Yale University Press), which argues that the world's supply of monetary gold is far too small to finance the expanding volume of international trade and finance, and *The U.S. Balance of Payments in 1968* (Washington: Brookings Institution), popularly known as the "Brookings Report," by Walter S. Salant *et al.*, which argues that inflation and economic growth will be so much more rapid in Western Europe than in the United States that the American balance of payments will essentially take care of itself without requiring major adjustments in our domestic economy.

ACKNOWLEDGMENTS

I am especially indebted to my friend and former co-author, Robert L. Heilbroner, for his help in the preparation of this book. Indeed, the original idea for the book was his, and it would never have been written without his encouragement and enthusiasm.

Professor Lawrence Ritter of New York University was good enough to read the manuscript with unusual care. His many useful suggestions are incorporated throughout these pages.

My friends and associates Gilbert Kaplan, Harold Edelstein, and James Karanfilian contributed constructive and helpful criticism. Indeed, all of my associates at Bernstein-Macaulay, Inc., were magnificently generous in helping to make this project a reality.

A special note of thanks is due also to Robert Bernstein and Richard Kislik of Random House for demonstrating the power of positive thinking.

Four kind and wise people with whom I worked in the more distant past taught me a good deal of whatever is of value in this book: John H. Williams, Emile Despres, Robert V. Roosa, and Abner Jackson. I take this occasion to express my gratitude to them.

Needless to say, none of those mentioned above is responsible for errors of fact or theory that I may have committed herein.

ABOUT THE AUTHOR

Peter L. Bernstein has had a long and impressive career in the field of Money and Banking. After graduating from Harvard College in 1940, *magna cum laude* and a member of Phi Beta Kappa, he spent two years at the Federal Reserve Bank of New York as research assistant to Dr. John H. Williams, who then headed the Research Department of the Bank. Following active service during World War II, he taught economics on the faculty of Williams College. For five years, he managed the bond portfolios of two New York City banks, as well as serving as a lending officer and manager of the foreign department. Since 1951, he has been Executive Vice-President of Bernstein-Macaulay, Inc., a nationally known investment counsel concern, supervising the security portfolios of individual and institutional investors. Mr. Bernstein also teaches economics at The New School for Social Research in New York.

He is the author of *The Price of Prosperity* (New York: Doubleday, 1962) and co-author with Robert L. Heilbroner of *A Primer on Government Spending* (New York: Random House, Inc., 1963). His articles have appeared in *The Harvard Business Review, The New York Times, The Nation, The New Republic, The Review of Economics and Statistics,* the *American Economic Review,* and other journals.